INTERPRETIVE
INTERACTIONISM

Applied Social Research Methods Series
Volume 16

Applied Social Research Methods Series

Series Editor:
LEONARD BICKMAN, Peabody College, Vanderbilt University
Series Associate Editor:
DEBRA ROG, National Institute of Mental Health

This series is designed to provide students and practicing professionals in the social sciences with relatively inexpensive softcover textbooks describing the major methods used in applied social research. Each text introduces the reader to the state of the art of that particular method and follows step-by-step procedures in its explanation. Each author describes the theory underlying the method to help the student understand the reasons for undertaking certain tasks. Current research is used to support the author's approach.

Volumes in this series:

INTERPRETIVE
INTERACTIONISM

Norman K. Denzin

Applied Social Research Methods Series
Volume 16

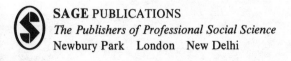

SAGE PUBLICATIONS
The Publishers of Professional Social Science
Newbury Park   London   New Delhi

For information address:

SAGE Publications, Inc.
2111 West Hillcrest Drive
Newbury Park, California 91320

HM
24
.D438
1989

SAGE Publications Ltd.
28 Banner Street
London EC1Y 8QE
England

SAGE Publications India Pvt. Ltd.
M-32 Market
Greater Kailash I
New Delhi 110 048 India

Printed in the United States of America

Library of Congress Cataloging-in-Publication Data

Denzin, Norman K.
    Interpretive interactionism / Norman K. Denzin.
        p. cm. — (Applied social research methods series ; v. 16)
    Bibliography: p.
    ISBN 0-8039-3002-X.   ISBN 0-8039-3003-8 (pbk.)
    1. Sociology—Methodology. 2. Social interaction. 3. Sociology—
—Biographical methods. 4. Participant observation. 5. Semiotics.
I. Title. II. Series.
HM24.D438 1989
301′.01′8—dc19   88-28246
                                                              CIP

CONTENTS

PREFACE

The rather considerable social science literature on qualitative research methods does not contain any extended treatment of the "interpretive," existential point of view (see Douglas and Johnson, 1977; Kotarba and Fontana, 1984). Nor is there any serious account that applies this perspective to the study of personal troubles and turning point moments in the lives of interacting individuals. The present work attempts to fill this void. It is designed to provide students and scholars in the human disciplines with a relatively accessible description of the existential, interpretive approach as it has been practiced by myself and others.

In *The Sociological Imagination*, C. Wright Mills (1959) challenged scholars in the human disciplines to develop a point of view and a methodological attitude that would allow them to examine how the private troubles of individuals, which occur within the immediate world of experience, are connected to public issues and to public responses to these troubles. Mills's sociological imagination was biographical, interactional, and historical. Despite the enormous influence of his work, there has never been a methodological discussion of how this theory and method might be put in place. This book continues Mills's project.

The perspective is termed "interpretive interactionism." By this rather awkward phrase, I refer to the attempt to make the world of problematic lived experience of ordinary people directly available to the reader. The interactionist interprets these worlds. The research methods of this approach include open-ended, creative interviewing; document analysis; semiotics; life-history; life-story; personal experience and self-story construction; participant observation; and thick description.

The term "interpretive interactionism," as the above list of methods suggests, signifies an attempt to join traditional symbolic interactionist thought (Blumer, 1969), with participant observation and ethnography (Becker, 1970; Lofland and Lofland, 1984; Adler and Adler, 1987; Agar, 1986; Fielding and Fielding, 1986), semiotics and fieldwork (Manning, 1987), postmodern ethnographic research (Turner and Bruner, 1986; Clifford and Marcus, 1986), naturalistic studies (Schatzman and Strauss, 1973; Lincoln and Guba, 1985; Patton, 1980), creative interviewing (Douglas, 1985), the case study method (Stake, 1986; Yin, 1985), the interpretive, hermeneutic, phenomenological works of Heidegger (1927 [1962], 1982) and Gadamer (1975), the cultural studies approach of Hall (1980), and recent feminist critiques of positivism (Cook and Fonow, 1986).

Those interested in acquiring a familiarity with the background of the present book might consult *The Research Act* (Denzin, 1978, 1989), *On Understanding Emotion* (Denzin, 1984), and my three studies of the American alcoholic (Denzin, 1987a, 1987b, 1987d).

THE ORGANIZATION OF THIS WORK

Interpretive Interactionism is organized in terms of seven chapters. Chapter 1 defines the approach. Its basic assumptions and terms are given. It is compared to more traditional, quantitative social science methodology. I also compare interpretive interactionism to the "Critical Theory" of the Frankfurt School, and indicate its affinities with recent feminist thought. I locate this perspective within the sociological tradition established by C. Wright Mills (1959) in *The Sociological Imagination*.

Chapter 2 discusses how meaningful, biographical experience is secured. Chapter 3 outlines the interpretive process. Chapter 4 addresses how the researcher situates an interpretive study. Chapter 5 analyzes thick description, and Chapter 6 shows how interpretation is done. Chapter 7 summarizes and presents the main conclusions of this study. It emphasizes the existential nature of this research. A glossary of terms is included at the end of the book.

Three assumptions organize this work. First, in the world of human experience, there is only interpretation. Second, it is a worthy goal to attempt to make these interpretations available to others. By so doing, understanding can be created. With better understandings come better applied programs for addressing the major social issues of our day. Third, all interpretations are unfinished and inconclusive. So it is with this book. It remains for the reader to form his or her interpretations of this project I call interpretive interactionism.

ACKNOWLEDGMENTS

I would like to thank the following persons for their assistance on this book. Leonard Bickman originally proposed the idea and guided me through proposals and successive revisions. Without him, it would never have been written. I was subjected to considerable pain at the hands of Debra J. Rog and Carl J. Couch. They destroyed my first and second drafts. I think this is a better book now, and if it is, they should take the credit. Conversations with David R. Maines clarified many of the ideas in Chapter 5. Robert Stake's comments on an earlier draft served to sharpen my position on the topic of qualitative evaluation studies. Graduate students in my 1988 course, at the University of Illinois, on "Writing Interpretation" helped me work through the arguments presented in Chapters 1 and 7. They were patient and insightful. Gary Krug, in particular, elaborated my understanding of the notion of "epiphany." I want to thank Richard Louisell and Wayne Woodward for their assistance with the proof reading and the construction of the index. Katherine E. Ryan, my wife, put up with my frustration and anger. Her good humor helped me stay with this project.

—*Norman K. Denzin*

1

The Interpretive Point of View

The essential features of interpretive interactionism as a perspective and method are defined. The following topics are discussed: (1) key terms; (2) the epiphany; (3) existential inquiry; (4) naturalism; (5) pure and applied interpretive research; (6) positivism and postpositivism; (7) gender, power, history, emotion, and knowledge; (8) the criteria of interpretation; (9) and the interpretive agenda.

This is a book about how to do interpretive interactionism as a mode of qualitative research. *Interpretive Interactionism* attempts to make the world of lived experience directly accessible to the reader. It endeavors to capture the voices, emotions, and actions of those studied. The focus of interpretive research is on those life experiences that radically alter and shape the meanings persons given to themselves and their experiences.

When to Use the Interpretive Approach

Three questions need to be addressed, before the reader turns to the body of Chapter 1. First, when should the interpretive approach be used? Second, how can this approach be used to evaluate programs that have been created to deal with "real life" problems? Third, how does the researcher go about doing this kind of research?

Interpretive interactionism is not for everyone. It is based on a research philosophy that is counter to much of the traditional scientific research tradition in the social sciences. Only persons drawn to the qualitative, interpretive approach are likely to use the methods and strategies I discuss in this book. Not all qualitative researchers will use the methods I propose. *The approach advocated in this book should only be used when the researcher wants to examine the relationship between personal troubles, for example wife-battering, or alcoholism, and the public policies and public institutions that have been created to address those personal problems.* Interpretive interactionism speaks to this interrelationship between private lives and public responses to personal troubles.

At the applied level, the interpretive approach can contribute to evaluation research in the following ways (see Becker, 1967, p. 23). First, it can help identify different definitions of the problem and the program being evaluated. It can show, for example, how battered wives interpret the shelters, hot lines, and public services that are made available to them by social welfare agencies. Through the use of personal experience stories and thick descriptions of lived experiences, the perspectives of clients and workers can be compared and contrasted.

Second, the assumptions, often belied by the facts of experience, that are held by various interested parties—policymakers, clients, welfare workers, on-line professionals—can be located and shown to be correct, or incorrect (Becker, 1967, p. 23). Third, strategic points of intervention into social situations can be identified. In such ways, the services of an agency and a program can be improved and evaluated. Fourth, it is possible to suggest "alternative moral points of view from which the problem," the policy, and the program can be interpreted and assessed (see Becker, 1967, pp. 23-24). Because of its emphasis on lived experience, the interpretive method suggests that programs must always be judged by and from the point of view of the persons most directly affected. Fifth, the limits of statistics and statistical evaluations can be exposed with the more qualitative, interpretive materials furnished by this approach. Its emphasis on the uniqueness of each life holds up the individual case as the measure of the effectiveness of all applied programs.

A basic thesis drives the applied focus of this book. It rests on the importance of interpretation and understanding as key features of social life. In social life, there is only interpretation. That is, everyday life revolves around persons interpreting and making judgments about their own and others' behaviors and experiences. Many times these interpretations and judgments are based on faulty, or incorrect, understandings. Persons, for instance, mistake their own experiences for the experiences of others. These interpretations are then formulated into social programs that are intended to alter and shape the lives of troubled people, for example, community services for the mentally ill or the homeless, treatment centers for alcoholics, medical services for AIDS patients. But often the understandings that these programs are based upon bear little relationship to the meanings, interpretations, and experience of the persons they are intended to serve. As a consequence, there is a gap or failure in understanding. The programs don't work because they are based on a failure to take the perspective and attitude of the person served. The human disciplines, and the applied social sciences, are under a mandate to clarify how interpretations and understandings are formulated, implemented, and given meaning in problematic, lived situations. Ideally, this knowledge can also be used to evaluate programs that have been put into place to assist troubled persons. *The perspectives and experiences of those persons who are served by applied programs must be grasped, interpreted, and understood if solid, effective, applied programs are to be created. This is the argument that organizes my book.*

How to Use Interpretive Interactionism

The method I develop involves the collection of thick descriptions and personal experience stories of problematic human interactions. These materials are then interpreted. Chapters 2 through 5 detail how this process works. It is basically quite simple. The researcher listens to, and records, the stories persons tell one another in groups. These stories are supplemented by open-ended, creative interviewing (Douglas, 1985). Thick descriptions and interpretations are generated out of these stories and accounts persons tell one another. There is nothing magical or mysterious about this method. It involves using skills any person already has; namely, the ability to talk and listen to others, including yourself, and remembering what you hear and what they tell you.

Interpretive research begins and ends with the biography and the self of the researcher. The events and troubles that are written about are ones the writer has already experienced or witnessed firsthand. As David Sudnow (1978, p. 154) argues, the individual's perspective is "definitionally critical for establishing the 'what'" and, I add, the "how" of problematic social experience. The task is to produce "richly detailed" descriptions and accounts of such experiences (Sudnow, 1978, p. 154). In this project, the writer has "no body but himself [and herself] to consult" (Sudnow, 1978, p. 154). Important consequences follow from this position. Only you can write your experiences. No one else can write them for you. No one else can write them better then you can. What you write is important.

Clarifying Terms

A number of terms need to be defined.

Interpretive: To explain the meaning of; the act of interpreting, or conferring meaning. *Interpreter*: One who interprets, or translates, meaning for others.

Interaction: To act on one another, to be capable of mutual action that is emergent. For human beings, interaction is symbolic, involving the use of language. Hence the term "symbolic interaction."

Problematic interaction: Interactional sequences that give primary meaning to the subject's life. Such experiences alter how persons define themselves, and their relations with others. In these moments, persons reveal personal character.

Interpretive interactionism: That point of view that confers meaning on problematic symbolic interaction.

Combing these terms, interpretive interactionists are interpreters of problematic, lived experiences involving symbolic interaction between two or more persons.

An Exemplar

Consider the following excerpt from Dostoyevsky's (1864 [1950, p. 71]) description of Raskolnikov's act of murder in *Crime and Punishment*:

His hands were fearfully weak, he felt them every moment growing more numb and more wooden. He was afraid he would let the axe slip and fall.... A sudden giddiness came over him.... He had not a minute more to lose. He pulled the axe quite out, swung it with both arms, scarcely conscious of himself, and almost without effort, almost mechanically, brought the blunt side down on her head.... The old woman was ... so short, the blow fell on top of her skull. She cried out, but very faintly ... he dealt her another blow... the blood gushed as from an overturned glass.... He stepped back ... trying all the time not to get smeared by the blood.

In this account, which is rich in descriptive detail, Dostoyevsky brings alive the moment of Raskolnikov's crime. He describes the thoughts and feelings of Raskolnikov as he acted. He describes the act in detail. He brings the reader into the situation. The remainder of Dostoyevsky's novel deals with the meanings of this crime for Raskolnikov. Interpretive interactionists seek to produce and interpret records like this.

THE INTERPRETIVE HERITAGE

The interpretive approach followed in this book is associated with the works of a number of different scholars, including Marx, Mead, James, Peirce, Dewey, Heidegger, Gadamer, Weber, Husserl, Sartre, Scheler, Merleau-Ponty, Schutz, Barthes, Derrida, Lacan, Geertz, Habermas, Hall, Blumer, Becker, Goffman, Garfinkel, and Strauss. It is present in a variety of disciplines: education, history, anthropology, psychology, sociology, political science, English and comparative literature, and philosophy, to list a few.

It goes by a variety of names, including interpretive anthropology, or sociology, hermeneutics, cultural studies, phenomenology, symbolic interactionism, ethnomethodology, the case study method, and Chicago School Sociology. Yet it would be a mistake to categorize all of these approaches under the single label of interpretive. There are as many differing interpretive perspectives in the social sciences as there are practitioners who utilize the critical, qualitative, naturalistic methodology that defines the approach.

Some aim for grounded theory. Others seek out generic processes and concepts. Some impose a grand theoretical structure upon the interpretive enterprise, seeking a totalizing theory of human societies, human actions, and human history. Still others formulate ideal types and assess their theory-interpretive work in terms of such concepts as empirical adequacy, empirical validity, and so on. Some eschew such subjective concepts as self, intention, meaning, and motive, and search only for invariant, publicly observable patterns of action. They seek to locate these patterns in the taken-for-granted structures of the everyday world of conversation and interaction. A book could be written in these several varieties of the interpretive approach in the human disciplines.

For obvious reasons, I have chosen not to write such a book. I offer, instead, *my* version of interpretation and give it the name "interpretive interactionism." This phrase signifies an attempt to join the traditional symbolic interactionist approach with the interpretive, phenomenological works of Heidegger and the tradition associated with hermeneutics. Interpretive interactionism also draws upon recent work in feminist social theory, postmodern theory, and the critical-biographical method formulated by C. W. Mills, Sartre, and Merleau-Ponty. It aims to build studies that make sense of the postmodern period (Mills, 1959; Baudrillard, 1983; Lyotard, 1984) of human experience.

OPENING UP THE
WORLD FOR INTERPRETATION

As a distinctly qualitative approach to social research, interpretive interactionism attempts to make the world of lived experience directly accessible to the reader. As indicated above, the focus of interpretive research is on those life experiences that radically alter and shape the meanings persons give to themselves and their life projects. This existential thrust (Sartre, 1943 [1956]) sets this research apart from other interpretive approaches that examine the more mundane, taken-for-granted properties and features of everyday life (Garfinkel, 1967; Goffman, 1974; Johnson, 1977, pp. 153-73; Douglas and Johnson, 1977, pp. vii-xv). It leads to a focus on the "epiphany."

The Subject's Experiences and the Epiphany

Those interactional moments that leave marks on people's lives, like the murder described above, have the potential for creating transformational experiences for the person. They are "epiphanies." In them, personal character is manifested and made apparent. By recording these experiences in detail, the researcher is able to illuminate the moments of crisis that occur in a person's life. They are often interpreted, both by the person and by others, as turning point experiences (Strauss, 1959). Having had this experience, the person is never again quite the same.

Perhaps an example will make this concept of the epiphany more apparent. In the Christian religion, the epiphany is a festival observed on January 6 commemorating the manifestation of Christ to the Gentiles in the persons of the Magi. In this sense, the epiphany is a manifestation or sign of the Christian deity. Now consider the following moment in the life of the late Martin Luther King, Jr. On the night of January 27, 1956, King, at the age of 26, had received several telephone threats on his life. Unable to sleep, doubting his place in the Montgomery bus boycott and his leadership position in the Southern Christian Leadership Conference, he sat alone at his kitchen table. He heard an inner voice that he identified as Jesus Christ.

King stated that "I heard the voice of Jesus. . . . He promised never to leave me, never to leave me alone." The historian Howell Raines (1986, p. 33) comments on the use of this episode in David J. Garrow's recent biography of King:

> Other biographers have noted this episode, but Mr. Garrow asks us to regard it as the transforming moment, the most important night in his life, the one he always would think back to in future years when the pressures seemed to be too great.

Raines notes that King returned again and again in his later life to this epiphany, referring to it as "the vision in the kitchen."

James Joyce's *Dubliners* employed this method of the epiphany. Indeed, he described his original notes for the book as epiphanies. Levin (1976, p. 18) discusses Joyce's use of this technique:

> Joyce underscored the ironic contrast between the manifestation that dazzled the Magi and the apparitions that manifest themselves on the streets of Dublin; he also suggested that these pathetic and sordid glimpses . . . offer a kind of revelation. As the part, significantly chosen, reveals the whole, a word or detail may be enough to exhibit a character or convey a situation.

The following passage from *Dubliners* reveals how Joyce (1976, pp. 108-9) uses this method.

> A very sullen-faced man . . . was full of smouldering anger and revengefulness. . . . He cursed everything. . . . His wife was a little sharp-faced woman who bullied her husband when he was sober and was bullied by him when he was drunk. . . . A little boy came down the stairs.
>
> —Who is that? said the man . . .
>
> —Me, pa . . .
>
> —Where's your mother? . . . What's for dinner? . . . You let the fire out! By God, I'll teach you to do that again!
> He . . . seized the walkingstick . . .—I'll teach you to let the fire out! . . . The little boy cried O, pa! and ran whimpering around the table, but the man . . . caught him striking at him viciously with the stick.— Take that you little whelp!

In this excerpt, Joyce reveals how the father's violence and anger are directed toward his child. In the interaction, the man's violent character is revealed.

Consider another form of family violence, wife-battering. Here is an example of an epiphany, as it is displayed in the life of a battered Korean wife. This woman is now separated from her husband.

> I have been beaten so many times severely in the early days of the marriage. But I would tell you the recent one. About 8 months ago, I was beaten badly. In the middle of the beating I ran out of the house. . . . But he followed and caught me. He grabbed my hair and dragged me to the house. He pushed me into the bathroom and kicked my body with his foot. My baby was crying. . . . Now I suffer from a severe headache. When I go out to the grocery store, I can't see items. I feel pain in my eyes. And I feel dizzy . . . I can't forgive him! I hate, hate, hate him so much. . . . Is this because I was born a woman? [Cho, 1987, p. 236].

Another battered wife describes her experiences in the following words:

He didn't let me sleep. We sat in the living room together from midnight till early in the morning. He forced me to sit down on the sofa while he drank beers. This went on for about a month. Everynight he said the same story. It was like to turn on the recorder. He said that I am a ruthless bitch. He said he doubted if I was a virgin when I married him. . . . In the early days of the marriage, he used to force me to be naked and then he drank looking at me. Then he told me to dance [Cho, 1987, p. 231].

In these excerpts, victims of family violence vividly report how they experienced battering. Their words bring the experience alive. These experiences became part of the turning point moments in their relations with their husbands. Cho (1987) has connected these experiences to the subsequent dissolution of these marriages.

Types of Epiphanies

There are four forms of the epiphany: the major, the cumulation, the minor and the illuminative, and the relived (see Chapter 7). In the major epiphany, an experience shatters a person's life, and makes it never the same again. Raskolnikov's act of murder is an example. The cumulative epiphany occurs as the result of a series of events that have built up in the person's life. A woman, after years of battering, murders her husband, or files for divorce. In the minor or illuminative epiphany, underlying tensions and problems in a situation or relationship are revealed. The account from Cho, given above, of the wife who was repeatedly battered by her husband, illustrates this form of the epiphany. As she stated, she had been beaten many times in the early days of her marriage. In the relived epiphany, a person relives, or goes through again, a major turning point moment in his or her life. The first wife above is reliving her last battering experience with her husband.

Locating the Epiphany

The epiphany occurs in those problematic interactional situations where the subject confronts and experiences a crisis. Often a personal trouble erupts into a public issue, as when a battered woman flees her home and calls the police, or an alcoholic enters a treatment center for alcoholism.

Epiphanies occur within the larger historical, institutional, and cultural arenas that surround a subject's life. The interpretive scholar seeks, as C.

Wright Mills (1959, p. 5) observed, to understand "the larger historical scene in terms of its meaning for the inner life and the external career of a variety of individuals." This asks the scholar to connect personal problems and personal troubles to larger social, public issues. Troubles are personal matters, like becoming an alcoholic, or being a battered wife. Issues have to do with public matters, and institutional structures like treatment centers for alcoholism, or shelters for battered women.

Troubles, Mills (1959, p. 8) states,

> occur within the character of the individual and within the range of his [her] immediate relations with others; they have to do with his [her] self and those limited areas of social life of which he [she] is directly and personally aware. . . . A trouble is a private matter: values cherished by an individual are felt by him [her] to be threatened.

Issues, on the other hand,

> have to do with matters that transcend these local environments of the individual and the range of his [her] inner life. They have to do with the organization of many such milieux into the institutions of an historical society as a whole. . . . An issue is a public matter: some value cherished by publics is felt to be threatened [Mills, 1959, p. 8].

Our task, Mills argues (1959, p. 226), is to learn how to relate public issues to personal troubles and to the problems of the individual life.

Troubles are always biographical. Public issues are always historical and structural. Biography and history thus join in the interpretive process. This process always connects an individual life and its troubles to a public historical social structure. Personal troubles erupt in moments of individual and collective crisis. They are illuminated, often in frightening detail in the epiphanies of a person's life. These existential crises and turning-point encounters thrust the person into the public arena. His or her problem becomes a public issue.

Strategically, the researcher locates epiphanies in those interactional situations where personal troubles become public issues. One works back from the public to the private, seeking out persons whose troubles have come to the public's attention. Cho (1987), for example, located battered women by going to a center for battered women in Seoul. My studies of alcoholism (Denzin, 1987a, 1987b) worked backward from treatment centers and Alcoholics Anonymous meetings to the personal lives of alcoholics.

Universal Singulars

Interpretive interactionism assumes that every human being is a universal singular (Sartre, 1981, p. ix). No individual is ever just an individual. He or she must be studied as a single instance of more universal social experiences and social processes. The person, Sartre (1981, p. ix) states, is "summed up and for this reason universalized by his epoch, he in turn resumes it by reproducing himself in it as a singularity." Every person is like every other person, but like no other person. Interpretive studies, with their focus on the epiphany, attempt to uncover this complex interrelationship between the universal and the singular, between private troubles and public issues in a person's life. In this way, all interpretive studies are biographical and historical. They are always fitted to the historical moment that surrounds the subject's life experiences.

WHAT IS INTERPRETIVE INTERACTIONISM?

Interpretive research has the following characteristics: (1) It is existential, interactional and biographical; (2) it is naturalistic; (3) it is based on sophisticated rigor; (4) it can be both pure and applied; (5) it is postpositivist and builds on feminist critiques of positivism; (6) it is concerned with the social construction of gender, power, knowledge, history, and emotion. A discussion of each of these points is required.

The Existential, Interactional Text

The interactional text (Goffman, 1983) is present whenever an individual is located in a social situation. It is ubiquitous. It is interaction itself. Interpretive studies collect and analyze existentially experienced, interactional texts. This is called doing existential ethnography (see Chapter 7).

The works of Goffman (1959, 1961, 1967, 1971, 1974, 1981) and Garfinkel (1967; Garfinkel et al., 1981) and their students are commonly associated with the study of face-to-face interaction and its interpretation. They have approached this topic from dramaturgical, linguistic, structural, cultural, and phenomenological perspectives. They have shown how the world in front of us can be read and interpreted in terms of the rituals and taken-for-granted meanings that are embedded in the interaction process. They have disrupted this order so as to expose its underlying normative assumptions. They have stressed its socially constructed nature and they have examined its fragile features. They have connected the micro world of interaction to the larger macro structures of society, including gender, race and ethnicity, work, medicine, psychiatry, science, play, and leisure.

There are four problems with this body of work, as it bears on the interpretive agenda. First it is nonbiographical and ahistorical. It does not locate interactional texts within the larger, historical social structure. Second, it seldom addresses existentially meaningful, or relevant, interactional experiences (but see Garfinkel, 1967, pp. 116-85; Goffman, 1961, 1967). Third, it inserts externally derived conceptual schemes into the reading of the interaction text. Fourth, it typically reads interaction texts in terms of broader structural and ritual issues. It seldom deals with the problem-at-hand, as these problems are addressed by the interactants in question. (These last two problems are often avoided by Garfinkel, especially when he deals with breaches or disruptions in interaction. They are prevalent throughout Goffman's works, however.) These authors adopt a structural, impersonal view of interactants and interaction. They study "moments and their men," not "men and women and their moments of interaction."

Ideographic and Nomothetic Research

Garfinkel's and Goffman's approach to the interaction text is *nomothetic* (Allport, 1942) and *etic* (Pike, 1954) and not *ideographic* (Allport, 1942) and *emic* (Pike, 1954; Denzin, 1984a, p. 182). Nomothetic studies seek abstract generalizations about phenomenon and often offer nonhistorical explanations. Etic investigations are external. They are often comparative and cross-cultural; they assume, that is, that the processes being studied transcend culture. Etic studies seek the discovery of general patterns. For Goffman, this might be face-work rituals, and for Garfinkel, the operation of the *et cetera* rule in conversations. Specific configurations of meaning that operate within a single case, or culture, are set aside in favor of cross-case universals.

Ideographic research assumes that each individual case is unique. This means that every interactional text is unique and shaped by the individuals who create it. This requires that the voices and actions of individuals must be heard and seen in the texts that are reported. Emic studies are also ideographic. They seek to study experience from within, through the use of thick description or accounts which attempt to capture the meanings and experiences of interacting individuals in problematic situations. They seek to uncover the conceptual categories persons use when they interact with one another and create meaningful experience. Emic investigations are particularizing. Etic research is generalizing.

Interpretive interactionist studies are ideographic and emic. They reject the nomothetic, etic impulse to abstract and generalize. For these reasons, there is only limited utility in the etic, nomothetic approaches to the interactional text taken by Goffman and Garfinkel. While their works establish the structural regularities present in interaction, their ahistorical, nonbiographical stance does not permit the discovery of what a particular interactional moment means to its interactants. Their ability to speak to the epiphany, or to the moment of existential crisis in a person's life, is thereby severely restricted. While they may be able to reveal the structure of such moments, they are unable to reveal their meanings to the participants in question.

The Progressive-Regressive Method of Sartre

For the above reasons, a different approach to the reading of the interactional text must be adopted. I have elsewhere advocated the use of Sartre's (1963, pp. 85-166) progressive-regressive method of analysis (see Denzin, 1984a, p. 183, 1986a, pp. 14-15). I have also termed this the "critical-interpretive method."

The progressive-regressive method seeks to situate and understand a particular class of subjects within a given historical moment. Progressively, the method looks forward to the conclusion of a set of acts or actions undertaken by a subject, such as Raskolnikov's act of murder or a Korean wife being battered. The term "progressive" refers here to the forward, temporal dimension of the interpretation process. Regressively, the method works back in time to the historical, cultural, and biographical conditions that moved the subject to take, or experience, the actions being studied. By moving forward and backward in time, the subject's projects and actions are situated in time and space. The unique features of the subject's life are illuminated in the interactional episodes that are studied. The similarities and commonalities shared with others are also revealed.

Naturalism

Interpretive interactionists employ a strategy of research that implements interpretive interactionism in concrete research and policymaking situations (see Majchrzak, 1984, p. 12; House, 1980; Stake, 1978; Lincoln and Guba, 1985, pp. 259-88; Patton, 1980, 1982). This method of research is naturalistic. It is located in the natural worlds of everyday, social interaction. It relies upon "sophisticated rigor" (Denzin, 1978, p. 167), which is a commitment to makes one's interpretive materials and methods as public as possible. Indeed, sophisticated rigor describes the work of any and all researchers who employ multiple methods, seek out diverse empirical situations, and attempt to develop interpretations grounded in the worlds of lived experience (Denzin, 1978, p. 167; Patton, 1980, p. 18). It builds out of the case study, biographical, ethnographic approach advocated by Stake (1978, 1986), Smith (1984) and others (see Denzin, 1989, chap. 8, for a review). It goes beyond the single-case method, to the analysis of multiple cases, life-stories, life-histories, and self-stories. It utilizes the full range of biographical-interpretive methods to be discussed in Chapter 2.

Types of Interpretive Researchers

There are two basic types of interpretive researchers. The first type, like Geertz (1973, 1983, 1988), Strauss (1987), and Becker (1986b), engages in *pure interpretation* for the purposes of building meaningful interpretations of social and cultural problematics. These scholars aim to construct interpretations that are grounded in social interaction. For example, Strauss's work on chronic illness and medical technology has as its goal a grounded theory that "accounts for a pattern of behavior which is relevant and problematic for those involved" (Strauss, 1987, p. 34). Becker's studies of how schools fail to teach students to learn are an example of pure interpretation that becomes evaluation (see Becker, 1986b, pp. 173-90). This kind of work (Strauss's and Becker's) can inform the second type of interpretive work, which is *interpretive evaluation*. Such researchers engage in policymaking research. They conduct research on "a fundamental social problem in order to provide policymakers with pragmatic, action-oriented recommendations for alleviating the problem" (Majchrzak, 1984, p. 12). Interpretive evaluation research is conducted from the point of view of the person experiencing the problem; it sides, not with policymakers, but with the underdog for whom policymakers make policies (Becker, 1973). This does not mean, however, that the point of view of the policymaker cannot be considered. This can be the case in those situations where others are criticizing and forming policy for policymakers (Stake, 1986).

What Interpretive Researchers Can Do

Research of this order can produce meaningful descriptions and interpretations of social processes. It can offer explanations of how certain conditions came into existence and persist. Interpretive evaluation research can also furnish the basis for realistic proposals concerning the improvement or removal of certain events, or problems (see Becker and Horowitz, 1986, p. 85). This mode of research may also expose and reveal the assumptions that support competing definitions of a problem (Becker, 1967).

Taking Sides

Interpretive evaluation researchers who do this kind of work are often partisans for one point of view (radical, conservative) while others becomes state counselors (they work for the government). Silverman (1985, p. 180) has discussed the problems with this latter approach, for often the sociologists becomes an agent of the state and is unable to conduct his or her research in a completely free fashion.

All researchers take sides, or are partisans for one point of view or another (Becker, 1967; Silverman, 1985). Value-free interpretive research is impossible. This is the case because every researcher brings preconceptions and interpretations to the problem being studied (Heidegger, 1962; Gadamer, 1975). The term *hermeneutical circle or situation* (Heidegger, 1962, p. 232) refers to this basic fact of research. All scholars are caught in the circle of interpretation. They can never be free of the hermeneutical situation. This means that scholars must state beforehand their prior interpretations of the phenomenon being investigated. Unless these meanings and values are clarified, their effects on subsequent interpretations remain clouded and often misunderstood.

Positivism and the Assumptions of Detached Research

Traditional sociological research, in its various forms (Patton, 1980), has assumed that social processes, experimentally and quasi-experimentally defined (Lieberson, 1985), have effects on real world affairs. These effects are assumed to be objectively measurable through the collection of quantitative data drawn from the world under study. By objectifying the observational process, this model divorces the researcher from the world under study.

This model presumes that social processes can be captured within the strict cause and effect paradigm of positivism (Lincoln and Guba, 1985, pp. 24-28), and quasi-experimentalism (Lieberson, 1985). This research paradigm assumes the following:

(1) "Objective" reality can be captured.
(2) The observer can be separated from what is observed.
(3) Observations and generalizations are free from situational and temporal constraints, that is, they are universally generalizable.
(4) Causality is linear, and there are no causes without effects, no effects without causes.
(5) Inquiry is value free (see Lincoln and Guba, 1985, p. 28, for a discussion of each of these points).

INTERPRETATION AND SCIENCE[1]

The interpretive perspective is deliberately nonpositivistic, or postpostivist (Lincoln and Guba, 1985, pp. 29-33). It opposes each of the above assumptions for the following reasons:

(1) Logical positivism and scientific sociology have historically assumed that the language of the natural sciences should and could be the language of the human sciences. This assumption held that references to the social world that could not be verified under quantifiable, observable, scientifically controlled conditions must—following Wittgenstein's (1922, p. 151) dictum—be "passed over in silence." Statements regarding human subjectivity, intentionality, and meaning were superficially treated, or excluded from the positivist's domain. Interpretive interactionism is founded on the study, expression, and interpretation of subjective human experience.

(2) Positivistic sociology seeks causal explanations of social phenomena. It does so through the use of a variable-analytic language that is largely divorced from everyday life. Interpretive interactionism rejects causal modes and methods of analysis. The search for causal "whys," causal paths, causal chains, and causal antecedents is detrimental to the study and understanding of directly lived experience.

(3) The "why" question is replaced by the "how" question. That is, how is social experience, or a sequence of social interaction, organized, perceived, and constructed by interacting individuals? How, then, not why.

(4) Positivistic sociology presupposes a theoretic-analytic conceptual framework that stands independent of the world of interacting individuals. This framework, whether derived from classical or contemporary theory (Marx, Durkheim, Simmel, Weber, Freud, Parsons, Merton, Habermas, or Homans), assumes that human behavior can be meaningfully categorized and analyzed within the conceptual elements of an abstract, grand, or middle-range theory. Directly lived reality drops out of positivistic sociology to be replaced by such complex variable terms as "base," "superstructure," "division of labor," "bureaucracy," "ego-function," "functional prerequisites," "distorted communication," or the "latent consequences of purposive action." These second-order concepts divorce human reality from the scientist's scheme of analysis.

(5) Interpretive interactionism aims, as much as possible, for a concept-free mode of discourse and expression. Its mode of expression is locked into the *first-order, primary, lived concepts of everyday life*. Following Merleau-Ponty (1973a), descriptive phenomenology, and interpretive interactionism, attempt to render understandable the "prose of the world." Such a rendering assumes that the streams of situations and experience that make up everyday life will not submit to experimental, statistical, comparative, or causal control and manipulation. Every human situation is novel, emergent, and filled with multiple, often conflicting, meanings and interpretations. The interpretivist attempts to capture the core of these meanings and contradictions. It is assumed that the languages of ordinary people can be used to explicate their experiences (see the analysis of Raskolnikov's crime in Denzin, 1982b).

Biography and Inquiry

This world does not stand still, nor will it conform to the scientist's logical schemes of analysis. It contains its own dialectic and its own internal logic. This meaning can only be discovered by the observer's participation in the world. The world does not stand independent of perception or observer organization. In these respects, interpretive interactionists find that their own worlds of experience are the proper subject matter of inquiry. Unlike the positivists, who separate themselves from the worlds they study, the interpretivists participate in the social world so as to understand and express more effectively its emergent properties and features.

Mills (1959, pp. 195-96) states this position in the following words:

The most admirable thinkers within the scholarly community . . . do not split their work from their lives. . . . What this means is that you must learn to use your life experiences in your intellectual work.

Interpretive interactionism asserts that meaningful interpretations of human experience can only come from those persons who have thoroughly immersed themselves in the phenomenon they wish to interpret and understand. There is, as Merleau-Ponty (1973a) argued, an inherent indeterminateness in the worlds of experience. Systems that attempt to resolve this indeterminateness by going outside the directly experienced realms of everyday life are simply inappropriate for interpretive purposes.

(6) The formulation of causal propositions that can be generalized to nonobserved populations (based on the extensive analysis of randomly selected samples) is a cardinal feature of much current social science work. The interpretivist rejects generalization as a goal and never aims to draw from randomly selected samples of human experience. This follows Stake's (1978, p. 5) position on this issue: "Case studies will often be the preferred method . . . because they are epistemologically in harmony with the reader's experience and thus to that person a natural basis for generalization." Interpretive researchers seek to build interpretations that call forth its readers naturalistic generalization. For the interpretist, any instance of problematic social interaction, if thickly described (Geertz, 1973), and connected to a personal trouble, represents a slice of experience that is proper subject matter for interpretive inquiry.

The slices, sequences, and instances of social interaction that are studied by the interpretivist carry layers of meaning, nuance, substance, and fabric, and these layers come in multiples and are often contra-dictory. Some flow from other people's histories, and some are of the person's own making. The knowledge and control structures that lie behind these meaning experiences must be uncovered in an interpretive investigation. Every topic of investigation must be seen as carrying its own logic, sense of order, structure, and meaning. Like a novelist or painter, the interpretivist moves the reader back and forth across the text of his or her prose. In so doing, the researcher makes recognizable and visible a slice of human experience that has been captured (see Sudnow, 1978, 1979).

The Feminist Critique of Positivism

The feminist critique of positivism (Farganis, 1986; Cook and Fonow, 1986) locates gender asymmetry at the center of the social world. It makes the doing of gender a basic focus of research (Garfinkel, 1967). The gender stratification system in any social situation creates dominance and power relations that typically reduce women to subordinate positions. The way this works must be studied. There is no gender-free knowledge. The feminist critique suggests that objective knowledge is not possible. It argues that knowledge should be used for emancipatory purposes. Feminist research, like interpretive interactionism, is biographical and naturalistic. It seeks to build upon recent developments in postmodern, poststructuralist social theory. Feminist research demands that the voices of women speak through the interpretive text.

To summarize, an understanding and interpretation of everyday life must consider the gendered, situated, structural, and practical features of that world. These points may be stated thus:

(1) Utilize multiple, case study, biographical methods.
(2) Find the crises and epiphanies in the subject's life.
(3) Connect these experiences, as personal troubles, to public issues and institutional formations.
(4) Employ sophisticated rigor.
(5) Present the phenomenon to be evaluated in the language, feelings, emotions, and actions of those being studied.
(6) Follow the five steps of interpretation, including deconstruction, capture, bracketing, construction, and contextualization (to be explored later in this chapter and in Chapter 2).
(7) Clearly state the researcher's value position on the phenomenon being evaluated.

Interpretive Criteria for Evaluation Studies

When the research project is an evaluation study, the following criteria should be added to the above list:

(1) Collect personal experience stories from the persons in charge of the program (volunteers, caregivers, paid professionals) and from the persons served by the program.

(2) Identify the different definitions (local and scientific) of the problem and the program under evaluation.

(3) Identify the moral biases that structure the definitions of the problem and the program.

(4) Identify the competing models of truth (rationality and emotionality) that operate in the setting.

(5) Collect thick descriptions of client, and caregiver, experiences.

(6) Formulate analytic and thick interpretations of the program, based on the local theories of each of the categories of persons in the situation.

(7) Formulate understandings of the program based on these interpretations.

(8) Compare and contrast local and scientific interpretations and understandings of the program.

(9) Show how statistical analyses distort and gloss the actual work of the program.

(10) Make proposals for change based on the fit between lived experiences (successes, failures) and the possibilities for change that exist within the program being evaluated.

These criteria allow researchers to evaluate one another's work. They also offer guidelines for organizing interpretive evaluation studies. They are value-laden and take the side of the client in any setting.

The process of interpretation is shaped by history, power, emotionality, and beliefs concerning knowledge. It is to these topics that I now turn.

HISTORY, POWER, EMOTION, AND KNOWLEDGE

History

History enters the research process in four ways. First, the events and processes that are studied unfold over time. In this sense, they have their own inner sense of history. Second, these events occur within a larger historical social structure. This structure shapes, influences, and constrains the processes under investigation. This structure includes language, in its various formations; micro and macro power relationships; and taken-for-granted cultural meanings that structure everyday social interactions and social experiences. Third, history operates at the level of individual history and personal biography. Each individual brings a personal history to the events that are under investigation.

Fourth, the researcher has a personal, historical relationship to the interpretive process. This has been noted above. This personal history also shapes research.

These four forms of history must be taken into account in any interpretive study. Too often the artificial constraints of research design ignore the temporal and historical dimensions of the phenomenon being interpreted. As a consequence, the research process becomes trivialized and artificial.

Power

History interacts with power and emotionality. Power permeates every structure of society. It is embedded in the micro, gender relations that makeup everyday life (Foucault, 1980). Power is force and domination. It may, in certain circumstances, take the form of violence. Power exists as a process, in the dominance relations between men and women, between groups and institutions. Power is force or interpersonal dominance actualized in human relationships through manipulation and control. It often involves the destruction of one human being by another. Power both creates and destroys. It creates new social formations while it destroys existing social structures. Recall, for example, the statements from the Korean wives battered by their husbands.

Interpretive research inevitably involves power. The researcher is often given power to enter a situation and make interpretations. In turn, he or she reports these interpretations to another who holds power over him or her. These interpretations often work their way back into the original situation. New social arrangements are implemented as a result.

Micro power relations permeate every aspect of research. They exist at the level of the researcher gaining access to the field situation so that observations can be made. They exist, as a matter of course, in the world that is studied, for it is structured and organized in terms of authority relations. They exist in terms of the research formats, observational methods, and experimental and quasi-experimental research designs the investigator employs. Science enters the research setting as power-in-practice. The researcher, that is, carries the power and prestige of science into the field.

Emotion

Close inspection reveals that emotionality is everywhere present in interpretive research. It is present in the moods and feelings persons bring to the study. It is present in the lives of those who are studied. It is present in the interactions that go on between researchers and subjects. It is present in the observations that are gathered. It is part of power and of being powerful, or powerless. An anatomy of power and feeling in the interpretive study reveals that detached, unemotional, purely cognitive interpretation is impossible.

Knowledge

Knowledge is a belief, or set of beliefs, about a particular segment of reality. Knowledge is socially and politically constructed. Knowledge is intimately related to power. Those who have power create and then define the situations where knowledge is applied. Those with power determine how knowledge about situations is to be gained. Those who have power determine how knowledge will be defined. Those who have power also define what is not knowledge. As Foucault states, "Knowledge derives not from some subject of knowledge but from the power relations that invest it. . . . All knowledge is political . . . knowledge has its conditions of possibility in power relations" (Foucault, 1980, p. 220).

Power and Interpretation

Under the positivist paradigm, quantitative, applied, and evaluative knowledge are assumed to be objectively valid. Once obtained, such knowledge is then assumed to have a real force and relevance in the applied social world. Under the interpretive paradigm, knowledge can be assumed neither to be objective nor to be valid in any objective sense. Rather, knowledge reflects interpretive structures, emotionality, and the power relations that permeate the situations being investigated. As a consequence, interpretive studies can only reveal the interpreted worlds of interacting individuals.

THE CRITERIA OF INTERPRETATION

In Chapter 2, I will outline the criteria by which interpretations are evaluated. They will be briefly reviewed here. These include the ability to illuminate the phenomenon, in a thickly contextualized manner, so as to reveal the historical, processual, and interactional features of the experience under study. Interpretation must engulf what is learned about the phenomenon and incorporate prior understandings while always remaining incomplete and unfinished.

These criteria for evaluating interpretations are put in place as the researcher moves through the five phases of the interpretive process. These are the phases of deconstruction, capture, bracketing, construction, and contextualization. *Deconstruction* involves a critical analysis and interpretation of prior studies of the phenomenon in question. *Capture* means that the researcher secures multiple, naturalistic instances of the experiences being studied. *Bracketing*, or *reduction*, leads the researcher to attempt to isolate the key or essential features of the processes under examination (i.e., the stages of being a battered wife). *Construction* describes the attempt to interpret the event or process fully, that is, putting together in a single case all the steps involved in being a battered wife. *Contextualization* occurs when the research locates the phenomenon back in the worlds of lived experience. Cho (1987, 1988), for example, located the instances of battering she had recorded back in the marriages of the Korean women she studied.

As the researcher enters the interpretive process, he or she is always located within the hermeneutic circle. The researcher, that is, can never get outside of the interpretive process. He or she is always part of what is being studied.

Situating Interpretation

In Chapters 3 and 4, I will examine how an interpretive study is situated in the natural social world. This includes finding and mapping the research site. It also involves connecting social types and biographies to research sites. The researcher must learn the language spoken in the field setting. The rituals and routines that structure interaction in the field setting must also be uncovered. Interpretation connects biographies to the interactions that occur within social groups.

Thick Description

Thick description attempts to rescue the meanings and experiences that have occurred in the field situation. It captures the interpretations persons bring to the events that have been recorded. It reports these interpretations as they unfold during the interaction. It establishes the grounds for thick interpretation. Thick interpretation attempts to uncover the means that inform and structure the subject's experiences. It interprets thick description. It takes the reader to the heart of the experience that is being interpreted. It assumes that all meaning is symbolic and operates at the surface and the deep, and the micro and the macro levels. It turns on thick description, which always joins biography to lived experience.

Interpretation and Understanding

Interpretation is the process of setting forth the meaning of an event or experience. Meaning is defined in terms of the intentions and actions of a person. It refers to the intended interpretation (and interpretant) of a symbol (Peirce, 1963, p. 108). Meaning is triadic. It involves interaction between (1) a person; (2) an object, event, or process; and (3) the action taken toward that object, event, or process (see Blumer, 1969, p. 9) Meaning is interactional and interpretive. Interpretation clarifies meaning. It may translate what is said in one language into the meanings and codes of another language. Interpretation brings out the meaning embedded in a text or slice of interaction. Understanding is the process of comprehending and grasping what has been interpreted in a situation or text (see Ricoeur, 1979, p. 96). Travelers in a foreign country, for instance, often cannot understand a request that is made of them until they are able to translate this request into their native language. In this simple example, the processes of interpretation and understanding are at work.

Two Types of Description

Description provides the framework for interpretation. That is, an act or process that is to be interpreted must first be described. A description may be thick or thin (Ryle, 1968, pp. 8-9). A thin description simply states facts. For example:

> X drank a cup of coffee at 8:00 a.m., on Tuesday November 24, 1987, while he wrote a letter to his publisher.

A thick description of the same action might read:

> X, while pouring his cup of coffee, remembered that his publisher had requested a letter concerning when his manuscript could be expected. Taking his coffee and cigarettes to his writing table, X began the letter, intending in it to state why he was late with his manuscript, and why a new deadline would have to be set. As he wrote the letter he was interrupted by a

phone call from his oldest daughter asking him how to insert a word into a computer text. He answered her question, and went back to writing the letter to the publisher. Angry because he had spent too much time on the letter, he dropped the excuses for being late and simply gave a new deadline.

A *thick description* has the following features: (1) It gives the context of an act; (2) it states the intentions and meanings that organize the action; (3) it traces the evolution and development of the act; (4) it presents the action as a text that can then be interpreted. A *thin description* simply reports facts, independent of intentions or the circumstances that surround an action.

Types of Interpretation

Interpretation creates the conditions for understanding. There are two forms of interpretation and understanding: the emotional and the cognitive. Emotionality and shared experience provide the conditions for deep, authentic understanding. It is this mode of understanding that interpretive interactionism attempts to build. Cognitive interpretations and understandings lay bare the essential meanings of a phenomenon, but they do not infuse those meanings with emotion. A mathematical formula, such as Einstein's Special Theory of Relativity, states relationships between phenomenon, but it does not give emotional meaning to these relations.

Thick description is the cornerstone of interpretation studies. Without it, authentic understanding would not be possible. This mode of deep understanding emerges as the investigator examines negative cases, or empirical irregularities.

THE AGENDA

The heart of interpretive interactionism lies in thick description, thick interpretation, and deep, authentic understanding. Explaining how to write documents that produce these phenomenon is the task of this book. The paucity of thick description in the interpretive literature is evident. This means that students must be taught how to do thick description and thick interpretation. At the present time, they are not taught how to do this, and this situation needs to be corrected.

At the same time, projects that utilize interpretive evaluation need to be undertaken. Such work will join the study of biography and society in ways that were outlined by Mills (1959). It will involve researchers drawing upon their own biographical experiences as they formulate their interpretive work. It will require an ability to think comparatively, historically, and interactionally. It will also dictate a consideration of the micro power, gendered relations that exist in the context that is being studied. This concern for power and for how power twists and shapes human experience gives interpretive research a critical thrust that is often absent in conventional evaluation studies. Interpretive studies should provide a thoroughgoing critique of the social structures and social processes that have been investigated. This will involve a critique of the general cultural formations that stand behind the phenomenon in question. It will also involve a critique of the intellectual-scientific thought that creates knowledge about the problem.

CONCLUSION

The several sides of interpretive interactionism have been sketched. After Mills (1959, p. 225), all interpretive studies must, as they draw to conclusion, orient themselves to "the terrible and magnificent world of human society in the last half of the twentieth century." The sociologist's voice can speak to this world. It can be more than a mere record of human experience. Paraphrasing Faulkner (Cowley, 1967, p. 724), it can become one of the props, the pillars, that help women and men endure and prevail. Our tests should display the agonies, the pains, the successes, and the deeply felt human emotions of love, dignity, pride, honor, and respect. This means, of course, that we have no claim over the lives, the experiences, and the stories we tell. We are interlopers. What is told us is given provisionally, if it is given at all. These lives and experiences remain, always, the lives and stories of those who have told them to us.

Final point: If one's goal is to understand and interpret the world as it is lived, experienced, and given meaning, then the strategies to be discussed in this book seem warranted.

NOTE

1. An earlier version of the arguments in this section is contained in pages 131-34 of my essay, "Interpretive Interactionism" (pp. 129-46 in *Beyond Method*, edited by G. Morgan; Beverly Hills, CA: Sage, 1983).

2

Securing Biographical Experience

This chapter takes up, in turn, the following topics: (1) Exemplars of problematic, biographical experience; (2) the biographical method and its relation to interpretive interactionism; and (3) the evaluation, reading, and interpretation of biographical materials.

EXEMPLARS

Consider the following story. It was told to the folklorist Sandra Dolby-Stahl, her sister, and her sister-in-law, by her mother, Loretta K. Dolby, as they were preparing food for a family picnic. The mother had been a fourth-grade teacher at a small rural school for nearly twenty years.

> It's just one of those dumb little things that you tell that doesn't amount to a hill of beans. Only, it was the last day of school and everybody was half crazy anyhow, trying to get everything done. And we had our principle and the P.E. instructor, the coach, there; they were goofing off. And I was sitting there trying my darndest to get everything caught up. And, everything wasn't going so well. And anyhow, I guess everyone was just sort of knowing what they were doing. These men met in the office there, and every once in a while I could hear them laughing. I knew they were telling dirty jokes and everything. And anyhow, we gals—they'd always shut up when we'd get anywhere close. So right at the end there, here the coach came down there, and he had two great big basketballs. And he *roll-ed* them clear down there, and they banged up against my door. And I came out of there and said, "What do you mean rolling your balls down the hall?" [laughter] Those guys—one went that way and one went the other. And pretty soon I heard them burst out laughing, and I went behind my door and slammed the door shut. And I didn't dare show my head out until they'd gone home. . . . Oh, I was embarrassed to death. Crimminee, when he banged those against the door, I came out and said the first thing that came to my mind. I didn't think it was funny til I realized how it sounded. But they vanished [Dolby-Stahl, 1985, pp. 55-56].

Now consider the following statement. The speaker is a 53-year-old printer at his second A.A. meeting in two years.

I can't get off the dammed stuff by myself. When dad died he made me promise that I'd quit. I promised him, but I can't seem to get to where I was when Dad died. The old man drank a quart of Old Fitzgerald every day for 30 years, then he quit cold when the doctor told him to. My sister's an alcoholic, she can't quit either. The boss says Frank you've got to quit. I try, but you know I get those shakes in the morning on the way to work. I stop and get a half-pint of Peppermint Schnapps, so they can't smell it on my breath, and I drink it and then I quiet down, start to smile, and feel good. It starts to wear off about the middle of the morning. That's why I keep the cold beer in the ice chest in the trunk of the car. I go out for a smoke and sneak a beer. That gets me through to noon. Then I take lunch at Buddie's and have a couple shots of Schnapps, with the beer that everybody else has. I can make it through the afternoon. Then I stop after work and really hit it. I get so shook up about not being able to stop that I seem to drink more. I keep drinking till I pass out every night. The wife understands, and when I mark the days off the calendar when I ain't had a drink she's so proud of me. I just think I ought to be able to do this thing by myself. The old man did. But I can't. I guess I'll just have to keep coming back to you people. My body's starting to show the effects now. The Doc says the liver can't take too much more of this. I don't know, when I take that drink these problems all go away. But they're there when the drink wears off. Can you people help me? [Denzin, 1987a, p. 25].

Next this:

It is by sheer force of work that I am able to silence my innate melancholy. But the old nature often reappears, the old nature that no one knows, the deep, always hidden wound [Sartre, 1981, p. x, quoting G. Flaubert, October 6, 1864].

The old wound is described below in a letter written about Flaubert by a family friend:

My grandmother had taught her elder son to read. She wanted to do as much for the second and set to work. Little Charlotte at Gustave's [Flaubert] side learned rapidly; he could not keep up, and after straining to understand these signs that meant nothing to him, he began to sob [Sartre, 1981, p. 3].

Finally, the following:

26 *April*: Mother is putting my new secondhand clothes in order. She prays now, she says that I may learn in my own life and away from home and friends what the heart is and what it feels. Amen. So be it. Welcome, O life! I

go to encounter for the millionth time the reality of my experience and to forge in the smithy of my soul the uncreated conscience of my race [Joyce, 1976, p. 526].

OVERVIEW

The subject matter of interpretive research is biographical experience. It is carved out of the lives of ordinary men and women. Interpretive studies, as argued in Chapter 1, are organized in terms of a biographically meaningful event, or moment, in a subject's life. This event, how it is experienced, how it is defined, and how it is woven through the multiple strands of the subject's life, constitutes the focus of interpretive research. (See Chapter 7 for further discussion of these types of events.)

Each of the above exemplars speak to biographically consequential moments in their speaker's lives. In the first account, Dolby-Stahl's mother recounts a sexually embarrassing experience as a schoolteacher. In the second story, the printer comes to A.A., asking for help for his alcoholism. In the third, Sartre describes a series of pivotal moments in Flaubert's life, and his slow entry into language. In the fourth, an excerpt from James Joyce's *The Portrait of the Artist as a Young Man,* Joyce conveys Stephen Dedalus's final thoughts as he turns his back on being a priest and departs Ireland for the Continent to become a writer.

In this chapter, I will return to these exemplars as I discuss the biographical method and its relationship to interpretive interactionism. I will distinguish the several forms of the biographical method, and then offer a detailed discussion of how interpretations are evaluated in interpretive studies.

CLARIFICATION OF TERMS

A family of terms must be defined. The biographical, interpretive method rests on the collection and analysis of stories, accounts, and narratives that speak to turning point moments in people's lives. A "narrative" is a *story* that tells a sequence of events that are significant for the *narrator* and his or her *audience*. A narrative as a story has a plot, a beginning, a middle, and an end. It has an internal logic that makes sense to the narrator. A narrative relates events in a temporal, causal sequence. Every narrative describes a sequence of events that have happened. Hence narratives are temporal productions (Culler, 1981, p. 187; Ricoeur, 1985,

p. 101). The content of a narrative exists independent of its telling, although many narratives can only be told by the person who experienced the events reported upon. Sandra Dolby-Stahl could not have told the story her mother told. Although, once hearing her mother's story, she can now tell it to anyone who will listen. Significant biographical experiences are told and retold in narrative form.

Types of Narrative

There are many different forms of narratives: stories in newspapers, and newsmagazines, short stories written by novelists, the stories people tell one another about themselves in everyday life, the stories people tell about other people. Interpretive researchers collect two basic types of narratives. A *personal experience story* is a narrative that relates the self of the teller to a significant set of personal experiences that have already occurred (see Dolby-Stahl, 1985). The story Dolby-Stahl's mother told about the "balls" is a personal experience narrative. The account of Flaubert's learning language is a second-person, personal experience story. It is told by another person about Flaubert. A *self-story* is a narrative that creates and interprets a structure of experience as it is being told. The printer's story is a self-story. He is explaining events and himself as he tells his story. Joyce's final words in *Portrait* are of the same category; he is explaining and interpreting events as they happen. Self-stories simultaneously deal with the past, the present, and the future. Personal experience stories deal with the past. Self-stories deal with ongoing problematic occurrences in the person's life.

Personal histories are reconstructions of a life based on interviews, conversations, and self- and personal experience stories (see Titon, 1980). They may be focused around the life, or biography, of a single person, group, or institution. Personal histories envelop and embed self- and personal experience stories within a larger narrative structure, that is, the story of a life. The full meaning of a personal experience or self-story can often only by gleaned by locating the story in the biography of the speaker. Dolby-Stahl, for example, interprets her mother's story by going into her biography and fuller life history. Sartre wrote two volumes on Flaubert, attempting to interpret the innate wound he felt throughout his life.

Process

The term "interpretive biographical method" will be used to encompass these variations on narratives and stories. The emphasis on self, biography, history, and experience must always work back and forth between a concern for process and the analysis of the specific lives of individuals who live the process that is being studied. The life of the storyteller must always be foremost in the account, or interpretation, that is written. Process and structure must be blended with lived experiences.

Following Paul Thompson (1978), interpretive, biographical materials may be presented in three different ways. First, single personal experience narratives may be presented and connected to the life-story of a given individual. Second, a collection of self- and personal experience stories may be collected and grouped around a common theme. Third, the researcher can offer a cross-case analysis of the materials that have been collected, paying more attention to the process being studied than to the persons whose lives are embedded in those processes.

It is recommended that all biographical-interpretive studies incorporate each of the above modes of presentation. Three implications follow. First, in-depth personal histories should be collected. Because any individual can tell multiple stories about his or her life, it must be understood that a life will consist of multiple narratives. No self- or personal experience story will encompass all the stories that can, or could, be told about a single life; nor will any personal history contain all the self-stories that could be told about that life's story. Second, multiple narratives, drawn from the self-stories of *many* individuals located in different points in the process being interpreted, must be secured. This triangulation, or combination, of biographical methods ensures that history, structure, and individuals receive fair and thorough consideration in any inquiry.

The Structuring of Lives

A life refers to the biographical experiences of a named person. A person is a cultural creation. Every culture, for example, has names for different types of persons: male, female, husband, wife, daughter, son, professor, student, and so on. These names are attached to persons. Persons build biographies around the experiences associated with these names, that is, old man, young man, divorced woman, only daughter, only son, and so on. These experiences have effects at two levels in a person's life. On the *surface level*, effects are barely felt. They are taken for granted and are nonproblematic, as when a person buys a newspaper at the corner grocery. Effects at the *deep level* cut to the inner core of the person's life and leave indelible marks on them. These are the epiphanies of a life. Interpretive researchers attempt to secure self- and personal experience stories that deal with events that have effects at the deep level of a person's life (see Denzin, 1986b, p. 324).

Each of the stories quoted at the beginning of this chapter speaks to events that had lasting effects on individual's lives. Several years after its occurrence, Dolby-Stahl's mother remembers the day she was embarrassed in the country school by the gym teacher. She shared this sexually embarrassing experience with her daughters and daughter-in-law. The printer tells about key life events that he is still dealing with. Joyce would write two more books making sense out of his relationship to literature and Ireland. Flaubert spent a lifetime struggling with his relationship to writing and language.

The above argument may be summarized in terms of the following points:

(1)   Epiphanies turn lives around.
(2)   Epiphanies have effects at the deep levels of lives.
(3)   Epiphanies are remembered, and personal experience stories are and can be told about them.
(4)   Epiphanies occur in problematic situations, such as a man raping his wife. These situations must be reconstructed and interpreted.
(5)   Epiphanies are group, interactional phenomenon.
(6)   These stories are given multiple meanings, by the person and others. Their meanings change over time.
(7)   Interpretive researchers collect and study deep-level personal experience stories.

Contextualizing Narratives: Interactional Slices

In addition to collecting narratives, interpretive researchers also record live interactional sequences. These sequences, if strategically selected, will be the occasion for the telling of personal experience stories.

"A 12-Step Call"

The following interactional recorded sequence was collected on January 23, 1983. It was reported to the author by one of the participants in the situation. The event occurred from 10:15 to 11:30 a.m. The settings were a motel room, an automobile, and a detoxification unit in a substance abuse center. The participants are three men: M., 34 years old, an alcoholic who has relapsed (gone on a drunk) and has called the A.A. hot line for help. P., a 43-year-old recovering alcoholic, and W., 50 years old, another recovering alcoholic who received M.'s telephone call. The interactants are sitting around a table in the detox unit. They have known one another for approximately eight months. P. and W. are doing what in A.A. is called a 12-Step Call. This means they are helping an alcoholic who has asked for help to stop drinking. They each have nearly one year of sobriety. The following conversation was recorded.

10:15 A.M.—	(Three men arrive at Detoxification Center)
M-P,W:	"Is that all there is? Is this what being in A.A. is all about?"
P-M:	"What do you mean?"
M-P,W:	(Reaches for a cigarette, hand shakes as he tries to light it). "I don't know. I mean, is this all there is? Go to your damned meetings, read your *Big Book*, not drink. Stay at home and take care of my mother. Is this all there is?"
W-M:	"No, there's more to it than that, but it has to start with not drinking. You can do anything you want to do. Anything. Just don't drink. Hell my whole life has turned around."
M-W,P:	"You can take your *Big Book* and throw it out the window. It don't mean nothin to me. I mean. IS THIS ALL THERE IS? My life's like that Peggy Lee song. It ain't got no meanin'. At least when I'm drunk I can be somebody else. I can get out of the old lady's house and be somethin'."
W-M:	"Will the *Big Book* help me stay sober. They got stories there just like mine and just like yours. Have you read it? Look at you now. You're drunk. Is this all there is?"
M-P,W:	"Man I can't take it. You know. I just can't take it. I think of my dead wife in San Diego. I see my mom waiting for me to come home drunk. I see myself in the bar having fun. I take a drink and I see A.A. faces in the glass. Man I just want to die."
P-M:	"It doesn't have to be this way M. It doesn't have to be this way. I felt the same way you do everytime I drank. Give A.A. a chance" [11:30 a.m.].

The conversation ends at this point. The two A.A. men leave the detox unit. M. is holding his head in his hands crying at the table. He has knocked over his cup of coffee.

The next day one of the speakers related the following story:

Yesterday I went on a 12-Step call. To a motel. I stayed at the same motel, once when I went on a week's drunk. It was good for me to go back to that place. To see what its like if you pick up that first drink. I was busy when the call came and I didn't want to go. But I'm glad I did. We got into the *Big Book*, into alcoholism and into my disease. I'm just glad I don't have to drink today. This was my first 12-Step call and I was scared as hell. There was a bottle of 4-Roses on the table and beer in the sink. Three months ago I would have had a drink. I'm sure. I don't think I'll ever forget how I felt in that room with that alcoholic who wanted our help. Empty beer cans, the smell of whiskey and stale cigarettes, cartoons on the TV. I'm grateful to be sober today.

Here an interactional experience becomes the occasion for a personal experience story. Interpretive research attempts to merge the study of ongoing interaction with the stories that come from such experiences. This is termed contextualizing a narrative.

Participating, Interviewing, and Listening

The interpretive interactionist attempts to live his or her way into the lives of those being investigated. He or she attempts to see the world and its problems as they are seen by the people who live inside them. As a strategy, this method throws the researcher directly into the social world under investigation. It requires the careful recording through field notes of the problematic and routine features of that world. Recurring structural, interactional, and meaning patterns are sought.

In some cases, the participant observer and ethnographer is a known observer. In others, the observer attempts to enter the world as a participant without disclosing observational intentions (Gold, 1958). In all cases, the researcher attempts to share in the subject's world, to participate directly in the rounds of activities that make up that world, and to see the world as the subjects see it. The participant observer's goals revolve around the attempt to render that world meaningful from the perspective of those studied.

Interviewing

Open-ended interviewing requires working from a general list of information that the researcher wants or from a set of questions for which the researcher wishes answers. Occasionally these questions are put to those studied in the manner of a focused interview (Merton and Kendall, 1946). The phrasing of the questions and the order in which they are asked are altered to fit each individual. Open-ended interviewing assumes that meanings, understandings, and interpretations cannot be standardized: They cannot be obtained with a formal, fixed-choice questionnaire. Open-ended interviewing assumes a skilled asker of questions, and it presumes skill in listening. The strategy fits naturally with participant observation, interactional study, and the collection of narratives. It is important to remember that a good interviewer is simply putting into practice what every good conversationalist knows how to do. An interview, that is, should be a conversation, a give-and-take between two persons. Douglas (1985, p. 15) has given the name "creative interviewing" to this process in which two or more persons creatively and openly share experiences with one another in a mutual search for greater self-understanding. This is how interviewing should be conceptualized and experienced. It should *not* be a relationship where one party does all the talking and the other only asks questions. When interviews turn into this form, they become asymmetric, authoritarian social relations in which the power of social science determines the information given (see Douglas, 1976; Couch, 1984, pp. 80-81, 186-87; Hall, 1985, pp. 314-15).

Listening

A good listener doesn't talk. He or she lets others talk. Interpretive research requires that the observer become a good listener. Several processes are involved in becoming a listener. First, one should not gossip. Second, a listener should not interrupt. Third, a listener should share experiences, thereby transforming the traditional interviewer-respondent situation into a sharing, conversational interaction. To listen only, without sharing, creates distrust. Fourth, the listener should learn what to listen for. Because personal experience stories and self-stories are sought, the researcher should learn how to be present in social groups and social situations when such stories are most likely to be told. Fifth, the listener has to have a reason for being a listener. This means that he or she has to create an identity in the social groups being studied.

Faulkner describes V. K. Ratliff, the narrator of his trilogy *The Hamlet* (1940), *The Town* (1957), and *The Mansion* (1959), as the person "who knew everything about folks in this country" (1940, p. 36), but who "didn't even tell himself what he is up to. . . . Not even if he was lying in bed with himself in the dark of the moon" (1940, p. 321). Ratliff was a traveling sewing machine salesman who called on every family in the county. He knew every family's life story. He knew the problems of every family. He knew who was in trouble and who wasn't. He never told one family what he knew about another. He was a trusted listener. He is a model for an interpretive researcher.

INTERPRETING THE BIOGRAPHICAL

Biographical materials must be interpreted. The following strategies are recommended. First, the subject, or case, must be located within the social group being studied, such as a recovering alcoholic, a mother telling a story, a writer trying to write. Second, the problematic act or event that structures his or her life must be identified and captured within a personal experience or self-story. Third, the basic features of the narrative must be interpreted. Fourth, these interpretations must be related back to the life in question. A brief discussion of each of these strategies is necessary.

Locating the Subject

Depending on one's study, subjects should be located easily. If they are having personal troubles, these troubles will take them to public institutions that deal with their problems. One needs only go to the institutional sites where the troubles are brought; there subjects will be found. Once found, they must be located within the social structure of the setting, that is, married, divorced, old, young, men, women, and so on. This means that the researcher must identify the categories and meanings that are used to define persons in that situation.

Securing Stories of the Problematic Event

Persons bring their troubling stories about problematic events in their lives to others. These others often make it their business to deal with such troubles. The printer, quoted above, brought his problems with alcohol to an A.A. group. The battered wives discussed in Chapter 1 brought their experiences to a shelter for battered women. The researcher listens and records the personal experience and self-stories that are told in these settings. These stories are then connected to the biographies of their tellers.

Reading the Narrative and Informed Readers

These narratives and stories must be interpreted. The interpreter of personal experience and self-stories must be an "informed reader" (Fish, 1980, pp. 48-49; Dolby-Stahl, 1985, p. 53). An informed reader has the following characteristics. He or she (1) knows the language that is used in the story, that is, what a 12-Step call is; (2) knows the biography of the storyteller, if only in a partial way; (3) is able to take the teller's perspective in the story; (4) has, hopefully, had experiences like those contained in the story; (5) is willing to take full responsibility for his or her interpretation; (6) is conversant with the full range of interpretive theories that could be brought to bear upon the story in question, that is, psychoanalytic, semiotic, poststructuralist, Marxist, feminist, interactionist, phenomenological; (7) assumes that "the creation of 'meaning' is the reader's response to the document he [or she] reads" (Dolby-Stahl, 1985, p. 52); (8) knows there is no one true, or real, meaning of a story (for a review of "reader-response" theory, see Tompkins, 1980); and (9) knows, nonetheless, that each teller of a story is the author of the story, and his or her meanings must be secured, if at all possible. I will illustrate these points by discussing Dolby-Stahl's (1985, pp. 58-60) reading of the "Balls Story" quoted at the beginning of this chapter.

"The Story of the Balls"

Dolby-Stahl heard the story as an informed reader. She knew her mother's personal history. She taught, at one time, in the same county where her mother taught. She attended the same church her mother attended. She was thoroughly conversant with the fact that a Church of the Brethren girl growing up in the 1920s knew about risque stories told by men and the language of sexuality. She knew that women who show an interest in sex are not ladies. But she heard in her mother's story a personal value that was counter to the value system of her culture. This was the value embodied in a woman telling a sexual story. Traditional values would have men, not women, telling sexual stories. But by telling the story, and by making the play on words with the pun "balls" (the two great basketballs banged against her door), the mother asserts that she has a right to "enjoy what has traditionally been regarded as masculine humor and to admit a real interest in sexuality" (Dolby-Stahl, 1985, p. 60).

Dolby-Stahl (1985, p. 62) argues that her informed reading of the "Balls Story" is "my truest perception of what she [her mother] believes. . . . a story such as 'The Balls' *functions* to teach the listener what the storyteller believes" (Dolby-Stahl, 1985, p. 62, emphasis in original). This assertion may be correct. It would be strengthened if the mother's interpretations had in fact been secured.

The Steps to Interpretation

Elsewhere (Denzin, 1984a, pp. 239-60), I suggested that the temporal work of interpretation, or hermeneutics, involves the following steps:

(1)   securing the interactional text;
(2)   displaying the text as a unit;
(3)   subdividing the text into key experiential units;
(4)   linguistic and interpretive analysis of each unit;
(5)   serial unfolding and interpretation of the meanings of the text to the participants;
(6)   development of working interpretations of the text;
(7)   checking these hypotheses against the subsequent portions of the text;
(8)   grasping the text as a totality; and
(9)   displaying the multiple interpretations that occur within the text.

Dolby-Stahl follows these steps. She offers the full narrative of the story. She subdivides the text into key units (the rolling of the balls, and so on). She performs an analysis of key phrases. She connects the meaning of these phrases to other phrases within the story. She develops working interpretations of the text, and checks these interpretations against other portions of the text. She treats the story as a totality, and places her interpretations against others that could have be given to it. This is how a biographical narrative is interpreted.

Going Back to Life

Dolby-Stahl connects her interpretation to her mother's biography. She uses this biographical knowledge to make sense of the story (her age, the Church of the Brethren, being a country school teacher in Indiana). By connecting a story to a biography, the researcher is able to show how interactional experiences make sense only when they are fit to the lives of their participants. If biography is ignored, empty, decontextualized interpretations are written. Dolby-Stahl, for example, could have read this as an instance of obscene folk humor in which "balls" would have been read as a slang term for testicles. This century-old usage of the pun by her mother would have then been coded into a standard folklore category and a "Freudian" reading of the dirty pun would have been given (Dolby-Stahl, 1985, p. 56). By linking her interpretation to her mother's personal history, Dolby-Stahl offers an informed reading that is thick and biographically relevant.

The Printer's Story

The self-story told by the printer at his second A.A. meeting can also be interpreted in terms of the above guidelines. The story reveals several problematics: getting off of alcohol, breaking a promise to his father, getting alcohol everyday, hiding how much he drinks, feeling like a failure. These problems are connected to his family situation. His sister is also an alcoholic. His father quit on his own. His wife understands what he is trying to do and supports him. He needs help and he asks if A.A. can provide it.

An informed reader would extract these points, and be able to compare this man's story to the stories other alcoholics tell at their first or second A.A. meeting (see Denzin, 1987b, chap. 4). He or she would learn more of the speaker's biography and attempt to understand how alcoholism has become a way of life for at least two generations of this family. An uninformed reader would simply offer an interpretation of the text, independent of these biographical facts. Informed readings attempt to treat each storyteller as a universal singular. This is what Dolby-Stahl did with her mother; Sartre, with Flaubert; and Joyce, with Stephen Dedalus.

CONCLUSIONS

In this chapter, I have indicated how biographical experience is studied. Personal experience and self-stories that focus on key turning point moments in people's lives are collected. These are fit to the personal histories of storytellers. Interactional slices are also collected and analyzed. Interpretive researchers learn how to become good listeners, as well as how to be ethnographic interviewers.

The interpretation of biographical materials requires that the researcher becomes an informed reader of stories and biographies. How this is done was outlined. In the next chapter, I discuss in greater detail the criteria for evaluating these interpretations.

3

The Interpretive Process

This chapter takes up the following topics: (1) framing the interpretive research question; ((2) detailing the steps of interpretation; and (3) outlining the criteria for evaluating interpretative materials.

THE STEPS TO INTERPRETATION

There are six phases or steps in the interpretive process. They may be stated as follows:

(1) framing the research question;
(2) deconstruction and critical analysis of prior conceptions of the phenomenon;
(3) capturing the phenomenon, including locating and situating it in the natural world and obtaining multiple instances of it;
(4) bracketing the phenomenon, reducing it to its essential elements, and cutting it loose from the natural world so that its essential structures and features may be uncovered;
(5) construction, or putting the phenomenon back together in terms of its essential parts, pieces, and structures; and
(6) contextualization, or relocating the phenomenon back in the natural social world.

A discussion of each of these steps is necessary.

FRAMING THE RESEARCH QUESTION

The research question is framed by two sources: the researcher and the subject. As indicated in Chapter 1, the researcher with the sociological imagination uses his or her life experiences as topics of inquiry.

The Sociological Imagination

The person with the sociological imagination thinks historically and biographically. He or she attempts to identify the varieties of men and women who prevail in a given historical period, such as the late 1980s and early 1990s in the United States (see Mills, 1959, p. 7). Such scholars attempt to examine "the major issues for publics and the key troubles for private individuals in our time" (Mills, 1959, p. 11). Persons with the sociological imagination self-consciously make their own experience part of their research. The sociological imagination is not just confined to sociologists. There is the "political imagination," the "psychological imagination," the "anthropological imagination," the "historical imagina- tion," and the "journalistic, or literary imagination" (see Mills, 1959, p. 19). What matters is the ability to think reflectively, historically, comparatively, and biographically.

The researcher is led to seek out subjects who have experienced the types of experiences the researcher seeks to understand. The subject in the interpretive study elaborates and further defines the problem that organizes research. Life experiences give greater substance and depth to the problem the researcher wishes to study. Given this interpretation of subjects and their relationship to the research question, the task of conceptualizing the phenomenon to be studied is easily given. It is contained within the self- and personal experience stories of the subject. The researcher seeks to uncover how the problematic act, or event, in question organizes and gives meaning to the persons studied.

The question that is framed must be a *how*, and not a *why*, question. As argued in Chapter 1, interpretive studies examine how problematic turning point experiences are organized, perceived, constructed, and given meaning by interacting individuals.

Framing the research question involves the following steps:

(1) Locate, within one's own personal history, the problematic biographical experience to be studied. Researchers work outward from their own biographies.
(2) Discover how this problem, as a private trouble, is, or is becoming a public issue that affects multiple lives, institutions, and social groups.
(3) Locate the institutional formations, or sites, where persons with these troubles do things together (Becker, 1986b).
(4) Begin to ask not why but how it is that these experiences occur.
(5) Attempt to formulate your research question into a single statement.

Exemplars: The Forms of Interaction

For the last two decades, Carl Couch and his students (see Couch, Saxton, and Katovich, 1986a, 1986b) have been formulating "how"

questions concerning the discovery of the "invariant sequences of interaction necessary for the construction of social forms" (Couch, Saxton,
and Katovich, 1986a, p. xviii). They have developed a complex and
dense body of audio-video recordings of social interaction in the small
groups laboratory. An informed, sociological understanding of the
elementary forms of social activity has emerged from this body of
research. Two factors separate this work from other social psychological laboratory studies of social interaction. The first is its focus
on the "how" and not the causal "why" question. The second is its
commitment to always study two or more persons, as dyads and triads,
doing things together. The "how" question must always be framed
interactionally. This is the case because the focus of interpretive is
always on "how people do things together" (Becker, 1986b). People
interact when they do things together.

Emotional Experience and the Alcoholic Self

In *On Understanding Emotion* (Denzin, 1984a), I focused on a single
"how" question. I asked: "How is emotion, as a form of consciousness,
lived, experienced, articulated and felt?" This lead to an examination of
classical and contemporary theories of emotion, an extended analysis of
the essence of emotional experience, and two case studies dealing with
family violence and emotionally divided selves. I attempted to answer
my "how" question by going to concrete situations where persons interactionally displayed violent emotions.

In *The Alcoholic Self* (Denzin, 1987a) and *The Recovering Alcoholic*
(Denzin, 1987b), I asked two "how" questions: "How do ordinary men
and women live and experience the alcoholic self active alcoholism
produces?" (Denzin, 1987a, p. 15); and "How is the recovering self of the
alcoholic lived into existence?" (Denzin, 1987b, p. 11). These two questions lead me to A.A., to alcoholic families, and to treatment centers for
alcoholism, where I found persons interactionally grappling with the
problematics contained in my two "how" questions.

Implementing the How Question

The how question is implemented in four ways. First, persons may be
brought to a research site, for example, Couch's laboratory. Once in the
site, they are studied naturalistically (Katovich, Saxton, and Powell,

1986). Second, researchers, as suggested above, may go to those places where persons with the experience naturally interact. Third, investigators may study their own interactional experiences. Fourth, the scientific, biographical, autobiographical, and fictional accounts that persons have given of their own, or others', experiences with the "how" question may be examined (Strauss, 1987). It is advised the researchers use as many of the above strategies as possible when they begin to implement their "how" questions. I turn now to the task of deconstruction.

DECONSTRUCTION

A deconstructive reading of a phenomenon involves a critical analysis of how it has been presented, studied, and analyzed in the existing research and theoretical literature (see Heidegger, 1982, p. 23; Derrida, 1981, pp. 35-36; Denzin, 1984a, p. 11). Deconstruction has the following characteristics:

(1)   It lays bare prior conceptions of the phenomenon in question. This includes how the phenomenon has been defined, observed, and analyzed.
(2)   A critical interpretation of previous definitions, observations, and analysis is then offered.
(3)   The underlying theoretical model of human action implied and used in prior studies is critically examined.
(4)   The preconceptions and biases that surround existing understanding are then presented.

I will offer two examples of deconstruction.

Exemplars: Battered Wives

Cho's (1987) social phenomenological analysis of Korean family violence provides an example of how deconstruction works. The major theory in the area is based on social exchange theory. This theory argues that violence is a normal part of family life and that husbands and wives seek to maximize rewards and minimize costs in their exchange relations. It argues that when the husband perceives an imbalance of exchange he becomes violent and uses physical force as a resource to restore equity in the relationship. The theory has been operationalized with a severity of violence scale that measures eight forms of violence:

(1) throwing things, (2) pushing and shoving, (3) slapping, (4) kicking and hitting, (5) hitting with something, (6) beating up, (7) threatening with a knife or gun, and (8) using a knife or gun.

The theory predicts that wives stay in violent relationships when the rewards are greater than the punishments. Wives leave when punishments are greater than the rewards. Cho argues that this framework has the following flaws: (1) It is tautological—there are no independent measures of rewards and costs, other than leaving and staying; (2) it contains no objective measure of the ratio of rewards and punishments; and (3) it contains no way of measuring a wife's subjective definitions of the situation. Hence the theory has no predictive or explanatory power.

Methodologically, this theory rests on the assumptions of positivism that were critiqued in Chapter 1. It assumes that family violence has an objective existence in family life that can be measured on a scale. It assumes that observations can be made, free of temporal and situational factors. It presumes a linear model of causality. The theory does not address subjective experience, or the interpretive process, that structures violent interaction (Denzin, 1984b). It views the wife as a passive agent in the violent marriage.

Cho's deconstructive reading of this literature followed the steps outlined above. She developed an interpretive interactionist view of family violence that was built from the accounts battered wives gave of their experiences.

The Alcoholic Self

In my study of the alcoholic (Denzin, 1987a), I devoted a chapter to modern behavioral science and its views of the alcoholic, alcoholism, controlled drinking by alcoholics, various theories of alcoholic treatment, and specific discussions of the alcoholic personality, craving, loss of control, and addiction as a scientific concept.

A number of biases or prejudices exist in this literature. It attempts to study alcoholism through positivistic procedures. Frequently, alcoholics are brought into the scientists' laboratory. There are few studies of alcoholics drinking or recovering in the natural settings of the social world. This literature, with few exceptions, ignores the experiences of problem drinkers. It approaches the phenomenon as if they were objects. The researchers attempt to develop procedures that would, or will, control the alcoholic's drinking. In this sense, the literature reflects a normative bias that drinking is good, if it is controlled.

This literature seldom attempts to take the point of view of the active or recovering alcoholic. It is written from the standpoint of modern, behavioral, objective science. The nature (or taken-for-granted) thesis that organized this research assumed that alcoholism was like any other phenomenon and hence could be studied experimentally, statistically, and in terms of the norms and canons of positivistic science. These studies attempted to answer causal or why questions. They infrequently examined how alcoholics experienced alcoholism. Various theories—learning, functional, psychoanalytic—are thus brought to bear upon the alcoholic's experience. There are few attempts to write and interpret that experience as it was lived and given meaning by alcoholics. This literature contains few explanations of slips; indeed, most recently (see Denzin, 1987b), it has focused on controlled drinking by alcoholics. (The works of Gregory Bateson, 1972, and H. Tiebout, 1944, 1954, are notable exceptions to this conclusion.)

By exposing these biases and prejudices in the existing literature, I was then able to locate my study within and against this body of work. This is the object of deconstruction. The scholar who builds upon my research would be required to perform a deconstructive reading of my position, for he or she may want to expose my biases and prejudices as these structured my interpretation of alcoholism and the alcoholic. It must be noted that no work is free of bias and prejudice (Gadamer, 1975). Every interpretation is prejudiced, or prejudges the phenomenon in question.

The hermeneutic circle. "Inquiry itself is the behavior of the questioner" (Heidegger, 1962, p. 24). The basic concepts and questions the investigator brings to a study are part of the research. They "determine the way in which we get an understanding beforehand of the subject-matter . . . every inquiry is guided beforehand by what is sought" (Heidegger, 1962, p. 24). An interpretive circle surrounds the research process. Heidegger (1962, p. 195) argues:

> This circle of understanding is not an orbit in which any random kind of knowledge may move . . . it is not to be reduced to the level of a vicious circle or even of a circle which is merely tolerated. . . . What is decisive is not to get out of the circle but to come into it the right way.

Interpretive research enters the hermeneutic circle by placing the researcher and the subject in the center of the research process. A double-hermeneutic or interpretive circle is implied. The subject who tells a self- or personal experience story is, of course, at the center of the life that is told about. The researcher who reads and interprets a self-story is at the center of his or her interpretation of that story. Two interpretive structures thus interface one another. Each circle overlaps to the degree that the researcher is able to live his or her way into the subject's personal experience and self-stories. These circles can never perfectly overlap for the subject's experiences will never be those of the researcher's. The best that can be hoped for is understanding. This point will be developed below.

CAPTURE

Capturing the phenomenon involves locating and situating what is to be studied in the natural world. Deconstruction deals with what has been done with the phenomenon in the past. Capture deals with what the researcher is doing with the phenomenon in the present, in his or her study. Capture involves the following:

(1) securing multiple cases and personal histories that embody the phenomenon in question;
(2) locating the crises and epiphanies of the lives of the persons being studied; and
(3) obtaining multiple personal and self-stories from the subjects in question concerning the topic or topics under investigation (Thompson, 1978).

Exemplars: Battered Wives

Cho (1987) collected personal experience stories from 64 Korean battered wives. She obtained her stories from an organization in Seoul, Korea, called the *Women's Hotline*, which received calls from battered wives from 10:00 to 6:00 on weekdays and 10:00 to 2:00 on Saturdays. Cho worked as a volunteer in the organization. She took calls from battered wives who she later held conversations with concerning their experiences. From these conversations emerged the personal experience stories that she analyzed in her study. (Two of these stories were excerpted in Chapter 1.)

The Alcoholic Self

In my study of the alcoholic self, I went to the places where alcoholics gathered. I presented myself as a person interested in A.A. I have alcoholic family members. I formed friendships with recovering alcoholics and their spouses and children. I also became friends with alcoholism counselors and other treatment personnel in treatment centers. I was able to listen to alcoholics talking in their homes, in public places where they drank, in hospital emergency rooms where they went for medical treatment, in detoxification centers, in treatment centers, and in A.A. meetings.

The "Printer's Story" and "The 12-Step Call" discussed in the last chapter are examples of the types of personal experience stories and interactions that I gathered in my study. Dolby-Stahl's "The Balls" story also illustrates an instance of capture, as do the earlier quotations from Sartre, Joyce, and Dostoyevsky.

Capture makes the phenomenon being studied available to the reader. It presents experiences as they occur, or as they have been reconstructed. When stories are to be grouped around a common theme, following Thompson's (1978; Denzin, 1986b) suggestions, multiple stories must be collected. This permits the researcher to compare and contrast the stories of many different individuals located in different phases of the experience under investigation. Multiple stories allow convergences in experience to be identified. Any story can be used, if it contributes to a general understanding of the phenomenon. Whenever using a story, however, the criteria for interpreting biographical material discussed in the last chapter must be followed. This includes locating the subject in the social world, reading stories as an informed reader, and connecting stories back to biographies. (This last issue is more properly the concern for contextualization. See the discussion below.)

BRACKETING

Bracketing is Husserl's (1913 [1962, p. 86]) term. In bracketing, the researcher holds the phenomenon up for serious inspection. It is taken out of the world where it occurs. It is taken apart and dissected. Its elements and essential structures are uncovered, defined, and analyzed. It is treated as a text or a document; that is, as an instance of the phenomenon that is being studied. It *is not* interpreted in terms of the standard meanings given to it by the existing literature. Those preconceptions, which were isolated in the deconstruction phase, are suspended and put aside during bracketing. In bracketing, the subject matter is confronted, as much as possible, on its own terms.

Bracketing involves the following steps, which parallel two of the steps in interpretation discussed in Chapter 2 (subdividing the text into key experiential units, and the interpretive analysis of each unit).

(1) Locate within the personal experience, or self-story, key phrases and statements that speak directly to the phenomenon in question.
(2) Interpret the meanings of these phrases, as an informed reader.
(3) Obtain the subject's interpretations of these phrases, if possible.
(4) Inspect these meanings for what they reveal about the essential, recurring features of the phenomenon being studied.
(5) Offer a tentative statement, or definition, of the phenomenon in terms of the essential recurring features identified in step 4.

Exemplars: The "Balls Story"

Dolby-Stahl offered a bracket interpretation of her mother's story. She took the text of the story apart. She interpreted key phrases. She then indicated how those phrases contributed to the essential, interpreted meaning of the story, for both her and for her mother.

The Printer's Story

In the last chapter, I extracted several general points from "The Printer's Story." I showed how his story spoke to general issues involving alcoholics, alcoholism, and addiction. I focused on the essential parts of his story as they revealed these features. I did not, however, locate the self-story and its features within the life of the alcoholic who was speaking. That is the problem of contextualization, which will be discussed below.

Battered Wives

Cho developed an interpretation of the centrality of resentment (ressentiment, see Scheler, 1912 [1961]) in the Korean family, based on her bracketed reading of the personal experience narratives of Korean battered wives. This interpretation argued that there are seven stages to resentment, once violence enters a marriage. These stages are (1) craving for genuine conjugal love, (2) rejection, (3) feelings of hatred, (4) feelings of revenge, (5) repression of revenge, (6) deep resentment, and (7) a secret craving for revenge. When a wife reaches this last stage, she harbors desires to kill her husband. A wife speaks:

Until he comes back at night, I can't sleep. I can't eat, I can't rest. I hate and hate. . . . For 14 years of our marriage, this feeling has built up. My nerve is so weak that I take a pill to rest. . . . I just want to kill him [Cho, 1987, p. 250].

Cho's bracketed reading of stories like this led her to develop the interpretation of resentment given above. Each of above terms (craving, love, hatred, revenge, desire to kill) were carefully defined by Cho in terms of actual statements made by Korean wives.

Bracketing and Semiotics

One strategy that assists in bracketing is the use of semiotics, a technique for reading the meaning of words and signs within narrative and interactional texts (see Barthes, 1972; Denzin, 1987c, pp. 1-20; Manning, 1987). A semiotic reading directs attention to the key words and terms that organize a text. It suggests that these terms (signs) are organized by a code, or a system of larger meanings. These meanings are, in turn, organized in terms of oppositions. The full meaning of a text unfolds as it is told or read. Two key types of signs within any text will be metaphors and metonymies. A metaphor ("He's as sharp as a tack"; "life is like a Peggy Lee song") suggests a resemblance based on analogy and simile. In metaphor, something is made to be like something else (sharp as a tack). That something else clarifies the thing to which it is compared. In metonymy, the name of one thing is used for another, such as bottle for drink, *Big Book* for sobriety, basketball for testicle. These two types of signs indicate how the words in a text can mean, or signify, more than they appear to mean on the surface.

A semiotic reading works from part to whole, and from whole to part. It uncovers the codes that organize a text, and examines the oppositions that structure its meaning. It alerts the reader to the use of metaphor and metonymy in the text. It draws attention to the multiple meanings of key words and utterances within interactional and narrative texts. It asks the analyst to perform both static and dynamic, or processual, readings of narratives.

A Semiotic Analysis of the "Balls Story"

Consider again the "Balls Story." The larger code that gives the story a meaning is a schoolteacher and mother telling a story about something that happened one day at a country school in Indiana. Within this code are phrases (P.E. teacher, coach, basketball) that have specific meanings in the code, such as coaches have basketballs. The oppositions that exist in the story deal with (1) men goofing off and women working, (2) male dirty talk and woman work talk, (3) dumb little things that are embarrassing to death, and (4) things that aren't funny that are later funny.

The key metonymy in the story revolves around the word "balls," great big basketballs, and the missing word "testicles." The meaning of the word "balls" is complex. It emerges from within the story, and includes their rolling against her door, her statement "what do you mean . . .," the men bursting out in laughter, her being embarrassed, realizing that the word "balls" carried a double meaning.

The mother's story, like all personal experience narratives, is doubly complex: First, the experience as it was lived was both funny and embarrassing. Second, the experience as told, is again funny, but now, in the telling, the mother distances herself from the original experience. Hence the original semiotic meanings of the story are not the same as those contained in its retelling. The first time through, the meanings turned on being embarrassed. Experienced immediately after they occurred, and in the retelling, they became funny.

The Limits of Semiotics

The double structure of a personal narrative points to the limitations of the semiotic strategy. A word, or sign, taken out of context has meanings that may not have been those experienced by persons in the situation. The metonymic meaning of "balls" changes with the telling.

Dolby-Stahl's interpretation of the story focused on each of the above dimensions. A semiotic framework would simply have made these interpretations more explicit. She would have explicitly organized her reading in terms of codes, oppositions, unfolding meaning, and metaphors and metonymies.

CONSTRUCTION

Construction builds on bracketing. It classifies, orders, and reassembles the phenomenon back into a coherent whole. If bracketing takes something apart, construction puts it back together. Construction involves the following:

(1) listing the bracketed elements of the phenomenon;
(2) ordering these elements as they occur within the process or experience;
(3) indicating how each element affects and relates to every other element in the process being studied; and
(4) concisely stating how the structures and parts of the phenomenon cohere into a totality.

Exemplars: Resentment in Violent Marriages

Cho's (1987, p. 249) seven features of resentment (ressentiment) in the violent marriage, which were identified, and defined, through the process of bracketing, were then contextualized in the following way. She states that in the beginning

> the wife craves ... love ... it is rejected by the husband's adultery ... the incidence of battering happens ... [she] begins to feel hatred toward the husband ... the hatred increases as the battering continues. She wants revenge ... the feelings of revenge are repressed ... ressentiment arises out of this situation ... her craving for revenge never stops ... the revenge plans ... [she] has in mind is not to end the relationship ... but to restore it with the punishment [Cho, 1987, p. 262].

In this contextualizing statement, Cho has created a processual definition and interpretation of resentment in the violent marriage. She has reassembled each of the elements in a sequential manner, indicating how each builds on and influences the other.

The Goal of Construction

The goal of construction is to re-create lived experience in terms of its constituent, analytic elements. Merleau-Ponty (1964, p. 62) describes this process in the following words. He is discussing the phenomenological study of emotion:

> One gathers together the lived facts involving emotion and tries to subsume them under one essential meaning in order to find the same conduct in all of them.

Replace the word "emotion" with "the phenomenon in question"—battered wives, alcoholism, sexual stories, murders, 12-Step Calls, leaving home—and Merleau-Ponty's injunctions still apply. The interpretive interactionist, in the phase of construction, endeavors to gather together the lived experiences that relate to and define the phenomenon under inspection. The goal is to find the same recurring forms of conduct, experience, and meaning in all of them. Construction lays the groundwork for the next step of interpretation, which is contextualization.

CONTEXTUALIZATION

Contextualization begins with the essential themes and structures disclosed in bracketing and construction. It attempts to interpret those structures and give them meaning by locating them back in the natural social world. For example, Cho located the resentment Korean wives felt toward their husbands back in their violent marriages. Contextualization takes what has been learned about the phenomenon, through bracketing, and fits that knowledge to the social world where it occurs. It brings phenomenon alive in the worlds of interacting individuals. Contextualizing locates the phenomenon in the personal biographies and social environments of the persons being studied. It isolates its meanings for them. It presents it in their terms, in their language, and in their emotions. It reveals how the phenomenon is experienced by ordinary people. It does this by thickly describing its occurrences in their world of interaction.

Contextualizing involves the following steps:

(1) Obtain and present personal experience and self-stories that embody, in full detail, the essential features of the phenomenon as constituted in the bracketing and construction phases of interpretation.
(2) Present contrasting stories, which will illuminate variations on the stages and forms of the process.
(3) Indicate how lived experiences alter and shape the essential features of the process.
(4) Compare and synthesize the main themes of these stories so that their differences may be brought together into a reformulated statement of the process.

Exemplars: Physical Contact and Violence in Sport

In an interpretive study of how women college basketball players experience physical contact and physical violence, Rail (forthcoming) has asked players to interpret game sequences in which contact, violence, and fouls occur. She has created a videotape biography of such sequences for everyone of the 14 players in her study. (The players were on the top-ranked women's varsity team in Canada in 1986-87.) She is attempting to understand and interpret the basic structures of physical contact and violence in women's varsity basketball. Here is a player describing her actions, as she views herself on videotape. She was not called for a foul.

> My intention was simply to go down in low post. Because I have a precise spot in low post. It's my place, it's my strong position. So, I know I have to be at a certain place to have an angle to go either on baseline or inside. . . . I have a spot I need to get at no matter what the defensive player will do . . . when I play defensively against a post, I know it's difficult to stop the post from going to her spot. So, contact, or not . . . in most cases . . . I'm ready for it. To play inside and not expect a contact, it's really rare [Rail, forthcoming, p. 26].

In this interpretation of a slice of experience, the player reveals an understanding of where she should be on the court if she is to get to her strong position. Seeing a picture of her body on the court, she indicates how contact is inevitable, interactional, and part of playing one's position. This statement contextualizes the phenomenon of physical contact. It locates it in an ongoing stream of experience. It is described, and given meaning, in the player's own words.

Here is the same player describing her actions in a different situation. A foul has been called on her.

> I was getting ready to go for the rebound, especially since I could see my defensive player going after the dribble. I told myself: great, I'll take my position. But . . . I took a bad position . . . I was totally under the basket . . . I was in disadvantage [Rail, forthcoming, p. 28].

The foul occurs because she took the wrong position under the basket and the referee called the contact.

These contrasting episodes reveal how the phenomenon of physical contact is shaped by interactional processes; in the last case, misreading one's position and the position of the defensive player under the basket.

The Goal of Contextualization

The intent of contextualization is to show how lived experience alters and shapes the phenomenon being studied. Whether the process is of being battered or fouling in a basketball game, the structures of the experience will be altered and shaped as they are experienced, described, and given meaning by their participants. Contextualization documents how this occurs.

EVALUATING INTERPRETIVE MATERIALS

Deconstruction, capture, bracketing, construction, and contextualizing bring into sharper focus the phenomenon under investigation. The goal of these interpretive activities, as indicated earlier, is to create a body of materials that will furnish the foundations for interpretation and understanding. Interpretation, as discussed in Chapter 1, clarifies the meaning of an experience. Interpretation lays the groundwork for understanding, which is the process of interpreting, knowing, and comprehending the meaning of an experience. Understanding, by locating meaning in the experiences of interacting individuals, is the goal of interpretive interactionism.

Ascertaining Meaning

The meaning of an experience, or event, as argued in Chapter 1, is established through a triadic, interactional process. It involves the person interpreting and acting toward an object, event, or process. This interpretive process brings the event or object into the person's field of experience, where it is acted upon and defined. These interpretations are reflected against the person's ongoing self-definitions. These definitions of self are emotional, cognitive, and interactional, involving feelings and actions taken in the situation. Meaning is biographical, emotional, and felt in the streams of experience of the person. Locating meaning in interaction involves uncovering how a person emotionally and biographically fits an experience into their emerging, unfolding definitions of self. It is assumed that this is done through the production of personal experience and self-stories. Meaning is anchored in the stories persons tell about themselves.

The following story is an example. The speaker has been sober and free of drugs for nearly eight months. He is speaking to a group of A.A. members.

I used to drug and drink with my old friends. We'd picnic and party. One time it went on for five days over the 4th of July. Now I don't drink or drug anymore and its like we haven't got anything in common. I mean now that I'm in recovery, my recovery means more than anything else to me. So its like I don't have these old friends anymore. I've only got friends in recovery now. I've got this customer. He tends bar. He keeps asking me to come by and have a drink. I can't tell him I'm an alcoholic and don't drink anymore. Its like I've lost this friend too. But man, I stand back and look at these people and look at me. Its like they're standin still, goin nowhere and I'm movin forward. They're back where I used to be. I'm glad I'm a recovering alcoholic and don't have to do that stuff anymore.

The meaning of recovery for this person is given in the above statements. He connects recovery to the loss of old friends and the gain of new ones. He connects his recovery as an alcoholic to his statements concerning where he is going and where his friends are. Meaning is given in his experiences.

Interpretive Criteria

Interpretive materials are evaluated in terms of the following criteria:

(1)   Do they illuminate the phenomenon as lived experience?
(2)   Are they based on thickly contextualized materials?
(3)   Are they historically and relationally grounded?
(4)   Are they processual and interactional?
(5)   Do they engulf what is known about the phenomenon?
(6)   Do they incorporate prior understandings of the phenomenon?
(7)   Do they cohere and produce understanding?
(8)   Are they unfinished?

Each of these questions requires brief discussion.

Illumination: An interpretation must illuminate or bring alive what is being studied. This can only be done when the interpretation is based on materials that come from the world of lived experience. Unless ordinary people speak, their experiences cannot be interpreted.

Thickly contextualized materials: Interpretations are built up out of events and experiences that are described in detail. Thickly contextualized materials are dense. They record experience as it occurs. They locate experience in social situations. They record thoughts, meanings, emotions, and actions. They speak from the subject's point of view.

Historical and relational: Interpretive materials must also be historical and relational. That is, they must unfold over time and they must record the significant social relationships that exist between the subjects being studied. Historically, or temporally, the materials must be presented as slices of ongoing interaction. They must also be located within lived history.

Process and interaction: These two dimensions should be clear. An interpretive account must be processual and interactional. Each example that has been offered thus far in the last three chapters has met these two criteria.

Engulfing: Engulfing involves including all that is known to be relevant about the phenomenon in question. This means that the interpreter must be an "informed reader," as argued in the last chapter, of the phenomenon in question. Engulfing expands the framework for interpretation. It attempts to exclude nothing that would be relevant for the interpretation and understanding that is being formulated. Because understanding and interpretation are temporal processes, what is regarded as important at one point may, at a later time, be judged not to be central. Interpretation and understanding are always unfinished and incomplete (see below).

Prior understandings: Engulfing merges with the problem of incorporating prior understanding into the interpretation of a segment of experience. Prior understandings would include background information and knowledge on a subject, concepts, hypotheses, and propositions contained in the research literature, and previously acquired information about the subject and his or her experiences. Nothing can be excluded, including how one judged the phenomenon at the outset of an investigation. This is the case because prior understandings shape what is seen, heard, written about, and interpreted. Hence prior understandings are part of what is interpreted. To exclude them is to risk biasing the interpretation in the direction of false objectivity.

Coherence and understanding: These two criteria ask if the interpretation produces an understanding of the experience that coalesces into a coherent, meaningful whole. A coherent interpretation includes all relevant information and prior understandings. It is based on materials that are historical, relational, processual, and interactional. A coherent interpretation is based on thickly described materials. The reader is led through the interpretation in a meaningful way. The grounds for the interpretation are given. The reader can then decide whether to agree or disagree with the interpretation that is offered.

Unfinished: All interpretations are unfinished, provisional, and incomplete (Denzin, 1984a, p. 9). They start anew when the researcher returns to the phenomenon. This means that interpretation is always conducted from within the hermeneutic circle. As one comes back to an experience and interprets it, prior interpretations and understandings shape what is now seen and interpreted. This does not mean that interpretation is inconclusive, for conclusions are always drawn. It only means that interpretation is never finished. To think otherwise is to foreclose one's interpretations before one begins. That is, individuals should not start a research project thinking that they will exhaust all that can be known about a phenomenon when they end their project.

CONCLUSIONS

In this chapter, I have discussed how the research question is formulated. I have shown how the phenomena to be studied are conceptualized within the worlds of lived experience. The steps and criteria of interpretation were also presented. Because the subject matter of interpretation studies is always biographical, the lives of ordinary men and women play a central place in the research texts that are created. It is, after all, their lives and their problems that are studied.

In a certain sense, interpretive studies hope to understand the subject better than she understands herself (Dilthey, 1900 [1976], pp. 259-60). Often interpretations are formed that subjects would not give to their actions. This is so because the researcher is often in a position to see things the subject cannot see. The full range of factors that play on individuals' experience is seldom apparent to them. The interpreter has access to a picture of the subject's life that the subject often lacks. The interpreter also has a method of interpretation that the subject seldom has (Denzin, 1984a, p. 257). The interpretations that are developed about a subject's life, however, must be understandable to the subject. If they are not, they are unacceptable.

4

Situating Interpretation

Any study of consequential, biographical experience must be located in the natural social world. This chapter examines the problems involved in situating an interpretive study. This discussion extends the analysis of "capture" offered in the last chapter. In capture, the researcher secures multiple cases and personal histories of persons who have experienced the problem or phenomena that are being studied. Personal history, personal experience, and self-stories are obtained from these individuals and then interpreted.

Situating, or locating, an interpretation involves the following steps: (1) determining when and where persons experiencing the problem come together and interact (these are the problems of timing, history, and mapping); (2) gaining access to the setting; (3) learning the languages and meanings that are spoken and employed in these situations; and (4) connecting individuals, biographies, and social types to the relevant situations of interaction.

TIMING, HISTORY, AND MAPPING

The researcher must connect persons to situations. I call this *temporal mapping*. It involves two interrelated processes: (1) determining the temporal sequencing and organizing of actions in the setting, and (2) locating settings and persons in space—that is, Where are these interactional situations located? Any social structure is made up of interacting individuals who come together in social situations. Persons bring and experience their personal troubles in such situations. In these settings, stories about personal troubles are told. These stories constitute the materials for interpretive studies.

Temporal Mapping

Temporal mapping focuses on *who* does *what* with *whom, when* and *where*. For example, the battered Korean wives in Cho's study came from middle-class marriages (the who). They called in and came to the Seoul hot line and told their stories to professional workers between the hours of 10:00 to 6:00 on weekdays and 10:00 to 2:00 on Saturdays. (Here, the "what" becomes storytelling; the "with whom," the professional listeners; and the "when" and "where," the hours and places just indicated.)

The process of mapping is important for several reasons. First, unless the researcher knows how the processes to be studied are distributed through the social structure, he or she risks studying atypical, or unrepresentative, instances of the phenomenon. Second, mapping builds a historical dimension into the research act. Every individual studied has a historical, biographical relationship to the event, crisis, or problem under investigation. (Mapping, in this sense, involves connecting individuals to situations. This will be discussed below under the topic of mapping individuals.) Third, the sites that are studied—that is, group meeting places, hot lines, places of work, violent homes, clinics, and so on—have their own histories within the social structure. This history has two dimensions. First, sites have histories with other sites (see the discussion below). Second, sites have their own histories (i.e., when they were established and so on).

The fourth reason temporal mapping is important deals with biography and personal experience. Temporal mapping is a process that every person, including the researcher, has to go through. Alcoholics, battered women, or basketball players have to learn when and where the interactions in which they participate take place. A battered woman can't call the hot line in Seoul unless she knows its office hours. An alcoholic can't tell her story to an A.A. group unless she knows when and where a meeting is taking place. The researcher's experiences will be like those of a battered wife, seeking help for the first time for her battering experiences. That is, the researcher must learn his or her way into and through the social structure in question. This is part of the process of living one's way into the phenomenon being interpreted.

Exemplars

In my A.A. study, there were old groups (started in the 1960s) and new groups (started in the 1980s). New groups took on ways of interacting from old groups. Indeed, in some cases, new groups were started by persons from the older groups. Personal experience stories told in new groups were shaped, in part, by the customs and traditions established nearly 30 years before in the original A.A. groups in the community. I would not have known this if I hadn't studied this historical relationship between sites. The second important historical dimension of a site refers to its history within the local social structure. Cho's Women's Hotline in Seoul, Korea, was established in 1983. It was the first such hot line for battered women in that city. Hence women who publicly told their stories of battering to a hot line did so for the first time to the workers in this agency. When a new site for dealing with personal troubles opens up in a social structure, it receives stories that it will not later receive when additional sites make their appearance. The telling of stories is shaped by the sites the social structure makes available for their telling.

Gaining Access and the
Stages to Temporal Mapping

Temporal mapping, which necessarily merges with gaining access, involves the following stages. These stages implement the process of capture (discussed in Chapter 3), and the problem of locating the subject (briefly discussed in Chapter 2):

(1) Identify the institutional site(s) where troubles are brought.
(2) Develop an explanation concerning your desire to be present in these sites and to study the interaction and experiences that go on within them (see Adler and Adler, 1987, pp. 39-43).
(3) Enumerate these sites, obtain their addresses, and determine the timetables that structure interaction in the sites.
(4) Write, as much as possible in this early stage, the history of the site and its relation (historical and interactional) to other sites.
(5) Determine who routinely comes to the site.
(6) Secure personal histories from established persons in the site.
(7) Begin listening for and collecting personal and self-stories concerning crises and epiphanies from the persons in the setting.
(8) Keep asking and refining the research question. This will involve asking and listening for "how" answers to the ways that the problem in question was and continues to be a personal trouble for the individuals (and groups) being studied.

Exemplars: Battered Wives

In Chapter 3, I discussed how Cho (1987) obtained her materials on battered wives in Seoul, Korea. She followed the eight steps outlined above. Her site was the Women's Hotline. Early in her study, she wrote a history of this facility and made a determination of who was using it. She obtained personal histories from the founders of the agency, and started collecting personal experience stories in her capacity as a telephone volunteer. She gained access to the setting (its hours were 10:00 to 6:00 on weekdays and 10:00 to 2:00 on Saturday), by immediately offering to work seven days a week from 9:00 to 7:00 doing secretarial chores including proofreading, serving coffee and fruit to the workers, and assisting in the preparation of case stories for newspaper columns. Within a month, she had become a staff member in the organization.

Alcoholic Selves and Their Stories

In my A.A. study, I went to the places where alcoholics and their families routinely gathered, including open A.A. meetings, which are "open" to anyone who has an interest in A.A. My research question, as noted in Chapter 3, involved, "How ordinary men and women experience active alcoholism and recovery." I collected personal experience and self-stories involving these two sides of the alcoholic's experience.

I addressed the problems and steps involved in temporal mapping in the following ways. At one of the first meetings I attended, I obtained a listing of all the A.A. meetings in the community. This listing gave the names of the groups, the times that they met, and their addresses. There were over 40 meetings a week, held either at 12:00 noon, or 8:00 p.m. I then started attending meetings. Over the course of three months, I was able to go to every meeting on the original list. Because A.A. members often go to three or more meetings a week, I soon found myself in different meetings with people I had met at other meetings. I became known as a person who went to many meetings.

I started to meet persons who helped get A.A. started in the community in the early 1960s. These persons were chairing meetings I attended. I had coffee with them. They talked about A.A.'s early beginnings and they told me when various groups first began to meet. These persons gave me histories of each A.A. group. They also told me who went to which meetings, who was having problems staying sober, who was doing well and so on.

While I was gathering the above information, I was learning how to listen to A.A. stories. I began collecting personal experience and self-stories from members as they spoke at various meetings. I also listened to recovery stories told after A.A. meetings when members went to local restaurants for coffee and dessert. In these ways I formed a working picture of the social structure of A.A. in the local community.

French Bakers

In their study of French bakers, and their wives, Daniel Bertaux and Isabelle Bertaux-Wiame (1981, pp. 169-89) utilized the life-story approach to determine how bakers and bakery workers work and live. They collected 30 life-stories from workers and 60 life-stories from bakers and their wives. They sought to determine the turning point experience that led bakery workers to become owners of bakeries. In France, 90% of the bread is still produced in local bakeries by over 45,000 artisanal bakers. The average baker and his wife work over 75 hours a week. The usual workday for the baker starts at 2:00 in the morning, and is finished at noon or 1:00 in the afternoon. Bakeries open for sales by 7:00 in the morning and stay open until 8:00 in the evening. Bakers' wives do the sales work, while the bakers make the bread.

Bakery workers in France (over 70,000) come from the provinces, where they are trained as apprentices. They come from peasant and lower-class families. They do an apprenticeship for seven years in the provinces and then many of them move to Paris where they work for city bakers. Only a small number of bakery workers ever become bakery owners. Bertaux and Bertaux-Wiame needed interviews with master-bakers, or bakers who owned their own shops. They also needed to study rural bakers and bakers in Paris. They obtained a list of Parisian bakers from their corporation-union in Paris; no such list existed for bakers in the provinces. They made contact with a province baker in the following way:

> While on holiday on the Pyrenees, Isabelle and I went to see the village baker. First we met the baker's wife.... When she understood we had not come to buy bread, she called her husband. He came, rather defiant, but as soon as we introduced ourselves as a couple of sociologists working together, they laughed and, interrupting us, commented that all told we were artisans just like themselves, only they were making bread and we were making research. . . . We did many interviews in this rural area [Bertaux and Bertaux-Wiame, 1981, pp. 180-81].

This is how they gained entre into the baker's world.

Here is how a bakery worker becomes a masterbaker. He works as an apprentice for a masterbaker. As this man nears retirement age, he begins to look for someone who will take over his bakery. This person must have two things: money to buy the bakery and a wife to work behind the counter. This man will have worked for the baker. The baker then offers him his shop for a certain price. The apprentice who isn't married at this time approaches a woman and asks her to marry him. If she agrees, he enters into a contract with the bakery owner to buy his bakery. Bertaux and Bertaux-Wiame (1981, pp. 184-85) describe this process:

> We noticed that several "self-made" bakers . . . told us they got married quite quickly (a few weeks after meeting their wife), and set up their own businesses even more quickly—sometimes right after the honeymoon. One of them made an interesting slip of the tongue. To the question "when did you marry?" he answered . . . I became self-employed, I mean I *got married* in 1966 [emphasis in original].

Workers delayed decisions to become self-employed if they could not find wives. New owners lost their bakeries if their wives did not adjust to the hard work of being a baker's wife. In one case, a young baker's wife

> used to close the shop at midday to have some time to herself, because she was not always good humoured, the largest bakery in a small town lost half of its customers to another bakery and the retired bakers lost most of their potential fortune . . . they lived upstairs and the old baker, unable to stand the rapid decline of his bakery, soon died [Bertaux and Bertaux-Wiame, 1981, p. 183].

This research example reveals how the life-story, interpretive approach can be fit to the problems of isolating the general structural and relational processes that shape key life experiences. The life-stories of the 90 men and women scattered throughout the French social structure that the Bertauxs collected revealed the history of this sector of production at "the level of sociostructural relationships" (p. 187). A single life-story, if understood, could have told the whole story. But the authors did not know this, until the end of their research.

LEARNING THE LANGUAGE AND ITS MEANINGS

As the researcher works his or her way into the research setting, the problem of language and meaning becomes important. Every group develops its own *ideolect* (Barthes, 1967) or special language. This language will contain certain terms and concepts that are not commonly spoken in other groups. It will contain special meanings attached to everyday words. It will also contain a code, or a set of rules, for putting words together. The language in this sense will have an institutional and historical heritage that must be uncovered. Because every group is a distinct language community, researchers must begin by learning the language that is spoken.

Steps to Learning a Language

Learning a language involves the following steps:

(1) isolating the key, recurring terms and phrases used in the setting;

(2) identifying how these terms are used by social types in the setting, including novices, newcomers, old-timers, men, and women;

(3) locating key printed and oral cultural texts that use these terms and phrases;

(4) isolating differences in meaning and usage, by site, gender, and length of time in the social structure and culture of the group;

(5) collecting stories and statements that contain these terms; and

(6) connecting these terms to personal experience, showing how their meanings and uses structure experience.

Learning a language takes time (see the discussion below).

Language and the Process of Understanding

Language structures and creates the processes of understanding and interpretation. As noted in Chapter 1, interpretation sets forth the meaning of an event, statement, or process. In understanding, a person grasps the meaning of what has been interpreted. Understanding and interpretation are emotional processes. They involve shared experience and shared meanings. Experiences cannot be shared if the language and the meanings that organize the experience are not understood. Shared linguistic understandings allow persons to construct common pasts and projected futures (Couch, 1984, p. 1). When a language and its meanings are shared, mutual understandings can be produced (see Couch, 1984, p. 38; Denzin, 1984a, p. 137). This is the case because persons can organize interactions that call forth in others common meanings, terms, and phrases (see Perinbanayagam, 1985). These phrases, and meanings, in turn, allow for the production of shared, meaningful experiences.

Exemplars: A.A.'s Language

In my A.A. study, I had to learn a new language. I followed the steps outlined above. I isolated key terms, began to note how different types of A.A. members used the words, began reading A.A.'s basic literature (*The Big Book, Twelve Steps and Twelve Traditions*), noted differences in the usage of the A.A. language, collected stories that used the language, and began to study how this language was connected to ongoing personal experience.

A.A. is a distinct linguistic community. It has special phrases, codes, terms, and meanings that are not immediately understandable to outsiders. Here are some examples: bottom, Dr. Bob, "How It Works," "home group," GSR, 12 & 12. When I first started attending meetings, I did not know what these words meant. I later learned that "bottom" referred to falling so low in life that one became ready to accept A.A. I learned that Dr. Bob was the cofounder of A.A. (Dr. Robert Smith), that "How It Works" referred to the reading of A.A.'s 12 steps at the beginning of a meeting, that GSR meant Group Service Representative, and 12 & 12 was *The Twelve Steps and The Twelve Traditions*.

Some of these words and terms are defined in the A.A. literature. Others are part of A.A. folklore and must be learned from A.A. members, or by listening to A.A. members talk. I learned what these words meant by reading the A.A. literature (Denzin, 1987a), and by listening to members talk in meetings. Without an understanding of them, I could not interpret what members were saying when they told their stories at meetings. Lacking this understanding, I could not participate in the shared A.A. experience (see the discussion below).

Novices, Newcomers, and Old-Timers

As A.A. gets inside the self of the alcoholics, these words become part of his or her A.A. vocabulary. As a member learns the A.A. language, he or she becomes part of the A.A. social structure. In A.A., there are at least four stages of language usage: novices (persons just exposed to A.A.), newcomers (persons who have made a commitment to become members), regulars (persons who have been coming at least a year), and old-timers (over 10 years' membership). In the following section, I will give examples of the language use of a novice, a newcomer, and an old-timer.

Novice

Consider the following self-story. It is made by an alcoholic in a treatment center. He is speaking to his counselor about the A.A. Steps.

> What the Hell is a Step!? Hell I can't even remember the numbers. How do I take the dammed things? How long does it take? When do I know I'm done? What's a..........Program? What do all these words mean? How can I meditate if I don't know what it means? What's a Higher Power? What's a defect of character? How do I made an amend? Christ I don't get any of this..........! ....what do I do? Help me [30-year-old salesman, in treatment for the first time].

This speaker evidences only a slight understanding of A.A. language. He does not know what Step, Program, Meditation, Higher Power, defect of character, or amend mean. Not knowing the taken-for-granted meanings of these terms and words, he is unable to apply them to his own experience. If he becomes a member of A.A., he will, over the course of time, learn what these words and terms mean. He will also begin to feel comfortable with the words.this

Newcomer

Compare the above statement to the following, made by a man who has been in A.A. for seven months.

> I read that story in the *Big Book*, 'The Vicious Circle.' That's me. I get sober a few days, then I drink and I can't stop. I've been here seven months and I have three months sobriety. I just couldn't stay stopped. Always something. Boss would yell at me. My mother'd be sick. The car wouldn't start. Green Bay would lose a football game. Any dammed excuse to go off and get drunk. I just about lost my good job. Today the boss is happy with me and everything goin' good. I finally got a sponsor and got me a regular set of meetings to go to. Its working for me. Last night, tho, I wanted to drink. My sister called and told me I was a quitter for stopping drinking. She's an alcoholic too. It scares her that I've quit. She wants me to keep drinking. Three months ago I would have gone out and drank a fifth over that call. Today I don't need to [Field conversation, January 10, 1985: 48-year-old mechanic, single].

This man is at a First Step Meeting. He is speaking to a newcomer who is at her first meeting. Seven months earlier, this speaker was a newcomer.

He has learned how to tell his story and he tells it as it is suggested in
A.A.'s *The Big Book*.

Old-Timer

Here is a speaker who had been in A.A. for over 30 years when he died
at the age of 76. He takes the framework for his story from A.A.'s (1976)
Big Book, which contains 44 life stories organized in terms of the
following statement: "Our stories disclose in a general way what we used
to be like, what happened, and what we are like now."

Bill Wilson could have told my story. Same circumstances. Bright
prospects for a prominent career in business. Good school, loving
parents, lovely wife, nice home. Everything. Heavy social drinking in the
early days. The best drinks, best bars and restaurants. The good life. But
the drinking got heavier. I was taking a bottle to work in my brief case.
Nips in the morning to get started. Early lunches so I could get a fix before
I started to shake too much. Then I started getting home late from work.
I'd stop for a few and a few would turn into all night. I became
irresponsible toward my family. My work started to show it. I wasn't
making the accounts like I used to. I decided I needed to switch jobs. So I
did and for awhile it was better. Then I started hitting the bottle more and
more. Some days I'd leave at noon. Sometimes I'd call in sick on Monday.
It got so I couldn't go longer than an hour without a drink. The wife left me
and took the kids. I said to "Hell with them," and I took an expensive
apartment in the city. Tried to live the bachelor life. I went down fast after
that. Started ending up in the drunk tanks. Went into a sanitorium to dry
out. Got drunk the day I got out. That was in the early 40's. People were
talking about this A.A. thing at the sanitorium. I read that Jack
Alexander article. A friend got a copy of the *Big Book* and gave it to me. I
looked at it and threw it away. Kept on drinking. I finally lost my job,
everything. Another place to dry out but this time when I came out I was
ready to stop. I got to an A.A. meeting and saw that *Big Book*. This time I
read it. It fit me to a "T." I knew I was an alcoholic. They said there was
hope if I followed their simple program. I started going to meetings. Got a
sponsor. Dried out, got sober. Got my old job back and after a year the
wife and kids came back. I've been in ever since. It turned my life around. I
owe everything to A.A. and to Bill Wilson, Dr. Sam Shoemaker, Dr. Bob
and all those oldtimers who held in there and kept A.A. going. In the early
days we used to drive 500 miles a week just to make meetings every night.
There weren't many then, you know. We all hung together and helped
each other. Just like you people are today [Field observation,
May 2, 1982].

Several points may be taken from these three stories. The third speaker presumes a knowledge of who Bill Wilson (the cofounder of A.A.) is. The second and third speakers assume a knowledge of *The Big Book*. Because Wilson virtually wrote *The Big Book*, when each man involves these two word phrases, he locates himself within the taken-for-granted history of A.A. The third speaker in fact identifies himself with Wilson in terms of the bright prospects of his business career, good school, loving parents, and so forth. He becomes Wilson as he talks. Indeed, as he tells his story, he tells a version of A.A.'s story in the United States. He thus draws his listeners into a central part of A.A.'s folklore as he talks.

The third speaker makes reference to A.A.'s simple Program. This term glosses, or includes, A.A.'s 12 Steps and its 12 Traditions. It also includes A.A.'s spiritual Program, which involves a Higher Power, daily meditation, prayer, the Serenity Prayer, the Fourth and Fifth Steps, carrying the message, and so on. The first speaker lacks an understanding of all of these terms and phrases. In short, by using the word "Program," the third man creates for his listeners a chain of meanings and associations that range across all of the A.A. Steps and Traditions. The word "Program" glosses all of these associations and meanings.

The third speaker's text is filled with A.A. history and the special meanings contained in A.A.'s language. The second speaker, only seven months in A.A., evinces a similar understanding of how the A.A. language works. His story also contains other references to the A.A. language including terms like "sobriety" (not drinking and working the Program) and "sponsor" (an A.A. member who helps the individual stay sober and work the Program).

Interpreting Language

As a linguistic process, interpretation involves both learning the language that is to be interpreted, and learning how to interpret that language once it has been learned. This is the point of the example of the salesman asking his counselor about the Steps. He has yet to learn the language that he is being asked to apply to himself. As a result, he cannot interpret what that language will do for him. More is involved. Learning how to interpret a language requires an examination of how that language is employed by the speaker in question. It requires a historical understanding of the language, the speaker, and the audience to which he or she is speaking. It requires an understanding of the range of meanings that can be meant when a term or phrase is used.

When a language has been learned and is then put into use, it begins to structure the experiences of the speaker. Language, in this sense, speaks for the speaker. It gives the speaker a set of terms that convey and capture meaningful experience in ways that other terms could not. This is what our salesman is struggling with. He does not know how to fit A.A.'s language to his experience. As a result, he cannot interpret his experience. He has confronted a wall and is asking for help.

Interpretive methodologists must learn and grasp this double structure that is embedded in language. They must learn the language that is spoken by those they study. They must then learn the possible uses to which that language can be put. In addition, they must learn how to read and decode that language once it takes the shape of a social text that is given in self-stories. Language, in this respect, is the gateway into the inner interpretive structures of the lives that are being studied (see Dougherty, 1985, pp. 4-9).

INDIVIDUALS, BIOGRAPHIES, AND SOCIAL TYPES

Not everybody uses or understands a language in the same way. This was the point of the above discussion, where I identified three different types of speakers of the A.A. language: novices, old-timers, and newcomers. The second step of learning a language (as indicated above) involves identifying how different types of people in the research site use the language. This requires two interrelated processes: (1) an identification of social types and (2) connecting individuals and biographies to situations of interaction. In this phase of situating interpretation, the researcher begins to classify and categorize biographical information.

Exemplar: A.A. Social Types

As the researcher gets deeper into the research situation, a picture of *social types* will slowly begin to take shape. A social type is an individual who represents through his or her actions a typical way of acting in a social situation (see Johnson, 1975, pp. 96-98, 122). A social type typifies (Schutz, 1964) a common way of presenting self, showing emotion, relating to others, talking, and putting into action the values and taken-for-granted meanings of a social group. Orin Klapp (1964) has analyzed a variety of different social types in American society, including the hero, the villain, and the fool. Klapp (1964, pp. 21-22) describes a social type in these words:

> A "social type" is a kind of person or role found in a certain milieu—for example, playboy, tightwad . . . it refers to a kind of character found in one or several occupational categories or social levels. Nor is it a personality type, in the sense of a psychologically adequate description of an individual, yet it does often refer to an outstanding trait accurately enough to identify individuals for people who know the milieu.

Klapp offers as examples of social types within Southern California high schools in the early 1960s, such as "surfer," "cool head," "brain," "soc.," and "ivy-leaguer." The social type exhibits behaviors and actions that make him (or her) easily identifiable within a social situation. The person-as-a-type is identified in terms of the values and taken-for-granted meanings of the group.

Within A.A., there are a number of different social types. These types display through their actions, speech, comportment, relations with others, and their sobriety histories various ways of being A.A. members. The following categories are used by A.A. members as they categorize one another. The newcomer to A.A. (and the researcher) will come to be able to identify the following types of individuals: (1) the newcomer, a temporary position; (2) the old-timer; (3) the "Dry" old-timer (a person who is hard to get along with); (4) the "Big Book" thumper or Step Person; (5) the "slipper" (the person who relapses frequently); (6) the person living on the street; (7) the "crazy" or the mentally ill member; (8) the "talker" (a person who talks longer then other members at meetings); (9) the "con" artist (a member who borrows money and doesn't repay); (10) the member on the "hunt" for members of the opposite sex; and (11) the loner, or person who makes few friends.

These social types will be differentially distributed through any A.A. community. There will be other types as well, and other ways of classifying members, including the person who has stopped smoking and can't stand smokers, the militant "anti-God" person, and so on. These types are fluid, a person can move from one category to another (newcomer to regular, regular to a person who slips or relapses, and so on). They define for the newcomer ways of being or not being an A.A. member. As newcomers learn this classification system, they modify it to fit their own experiences. These persons-as-types represent unique typifications of the A.A. experience. These types "structure" the initial and subsequent meanings and interpretations the person forms of A.A.

A member can only learn about these types by attending meetings and becoming part of the local A.A. culture. A member must learn how to see and identify these types, for each type-as-an-individual represents a different way of being an "alcoholic" in A.A.

Interpreting and Interrelating
Biographies and Social Types

These types talk the A.A. language. The member learns this language by listening to these different types of individuals talking and telling their A.A. stories. With greater A.A. experience, each type dissolves, or disappears, to be replaced by biographically specific information about each individual. The following conversation between an old-timer and a newcomer reveals how this works. The two members are discussing B., a regular around certain A.A. meetings who often acts in a manic way.

> Old-timer: Don't worry about B., he's as sweet as pie. He wouldn't harm a fly. He has a good Program. When he takes his medicine he's just fine. He just forgets to take it sometimes and he gets like this. He knows the Program, he does service work. He just has bad days and today is one of them.

A.A. social types will be differentially located, or distributed, throughout the A.A. social structure. To the extent that there is a class-based stratification system within A.A., certain types will be more likely to locate themselves at those types of meetings most congenial to their class position.

There is also a sobriety-based stratification system in A.A. Certain groups have a majority of members with less than one year of sobriety. Other groups will be made up of members with long-term sobriety. A mobility pattern joins these two stratification systems. Middle-class members who are newcomers may start out in groups where there is little sobriety, and then, when they obtain a year's sobriety, transfer their membership to a more solidly based middle-class group. An intersection of group history, personal biography, and the mapping of A.A. groups within a local community occurs in this process.

The researcher in this phase, as the A.A. example suggests, locates social types within the social structure being studied. The identification of these types leads the researcher farther into the social world being studied. They must then be connected to individuals who interact in particular social situations. This is the next topic.

CONNECTING INDIVIDUALS TO
INTERACTIONAL SITUATIONS

The above conversation reveals how a newcomer comes to acquire greater knowledge about a fellow A.A. member. As this process of learning unfolds, the member (like the researcher), learns to connect types, individuals, and biographies to situations of interaction. This is the last stage of situating the research. In this step, the researcher connects individuals to situations and groups. Typically, however, the mapping of individuals cannot occur until after the relevant situations in the social structure have been identified. This is the case because the researcher knows few people in the collectivity to be studied.

Connecting persons to situations builds upon the knowledge gained during the stage of temporal mapping. In this earlier stage, the researcher has determined who does what with whom, when and where. In order to obtain this knowledge, the investigator must become a regular in the situations where the members of the group routinely interact. This involves a process of connecting biographical history to social situations.

Exemplar: Learning the A.A. Social Structure

Here is how the A.A. social structure is revealed to the newcomer. By going to different meetings, he or she begins to recognize faces and names. He or she sees persons who have been present at other meetings. Soon it becomes clear that these familiar faces are people who go to X, Y, and Z A.A. meetings on a regular basis. The member learns to connect these persons to these meetings. They have mapped individuals to groups.

A newcomer speaking to a regular A.A. member:

Christ, I see you at every meeting I go to (the newcomer has been to three meetings in two weeks). Do you go to every meeting in town? You must keep pretty busy. Are you going to be at Friday Night at the Open Meeting? Can I bring the wife?

This newcomer is like the researcher studying A.A. He is learning how to connect persons to groups. The researcher must follow the same process.

A.A. directs the newcomer to attend 90 meetings in 90 days. This rule is seldom followed, but when it is, the newcomer soon learns who the regulars are in every meeting in the community. An elder A.A. member is speaking to a newcomer:

> Go to all the different groups. Go to Monday Night. Take the wife. She can go to Al-Anon. Try Tuesday Nights in _____ and _____ (the meetings in the small towns), try Tuesday Night at _____. Make the Wednesday Night Church Meeting. It has good sobriety. On Thursday you can go to the club, or _____. On Friday, try _____ or the Hospital, or the Gay-Lesbian, or the Open meeting. We have a lot of meetings on Friday night. I used to drink on payday. That's Friday. You better find a Friday Night meeting. Try out all of these meetings. On Saturday take the wife to the open meeting at the Treatment Center, or if you might want try that little closed meeting at _____. On Sunday give the Church meeting a shot. You need to make five or so meetings a week. So look around, try out the groups. You'll find people who tell your story. Get close to them. They may be willing to be your sponsor. Find yourself a home group and a set of other meetings that work for you. Make the meetings you have to stay sober.

If this member follows the directions that have been given, he will attend most of the A.A. groups in the community. It will take him several weeks to do this, but at the end of that time he will have encountered the majority of the regular A.A. members in the community.

RESEARCHER AS NEWCOMER AND THE KNOWING SUBJECT

The researcher is like the A.A. newcomer. He or she must learn how to map a social structure so that individuals can be connected to situations. Like the newcomer, the investigator must learn a new language and learn how to apply that language to personal experience.

The researcher seeks to become a knowledgeable member of the social structure being studied. He or she seeks to know what the typical member of the group knows. But more is sought. The researcher wants to know everything that is relevant so that thick interpretations of personal experience stories can be formulated. This means the researcher wants to be an all-knowing subject in the situation. Is this possible? Is there ever an all-knowing subject, or a person who knows everything that is relevant in a situation? The answer, of course, is no. Critical theorists like Habermas, Marcuse, Adorno, and Horkheimer (see Bottomore, 1984) have discussed this problem and argued for the creation of social structures where meaningful, undistorted human communication could occur. In such social structures, knowing subjects would exist, for they would have access to and understand what forces shape and impinge upon their experiences.

An all-knowing subject is a fiction. The best that the researcher can hope for are reflective subjects who can tell their stories and the stories of others. The researcher, like the subject, is always in the hermeneutic circle, always seeing situations and structures in terms of prior understandings and prior interpretations. Full, objective, all-encompassing knowledge of a subject or a situation is never possible. This problem will be taken up in greater detail in later chapters.

CONCLUSIONS

In this chapter, I have taken up the four steps that are involved in situating an interpretive study. These were discussed in terms of the problems of temporal mapping, gaining access to settings, learning a language, and connecting individuals, biographies, and social types to situations of interaction. Examples from several different research sites were discussed. I likened the researcher to a newcomer in a social group.

Interpretive studies examine how social groups and social structures create the conditions for the experiencing and expression of personal troubles. The discussion thus comes full circle. The original research site, whether it is an A.A. meeting, a women's hot line, or a baker's shop in France, must always be seen in terms of the histories that stand behind that social structure. The members who make up the structure have been discussed in terms of social types. These social types have, in turn, been found to have their own histories, located in the biographies of other group members. The interpretive study once again becomes historical as it attempts to interpret the relationship between individuals, turning point social experiences, personal experience stories, and social groups.

5

Thick Description

Thick description is the topic of this chapter. Description is the art of describing or giving an account of something in words. In interpretive studies, thick descriptions are deep, dense, detailed accounts of problematic experiences. These accounts often state the intentions and meanings that organize an action. Thin descriptions, by contrast, lack detail, and simply report facts. They are also called glosses. In this chapter, I compare these forms of description. Examples of both types are given and their relationship to thick interpretation is specified.

WHAT THICK DESCRIPTION DOES

Interpretive interactionism seeks to bring lived experience before the reader. A major goal is to create a text that permits a willing reader to share vicariously in the experiences that have been captured. When this occurs, the reader can naturalistically generalize (Stake, 1978, p. 5) his or her experiences to those that have been captured. This is what thick description does. It creates verisimilitude. It captures and records the voices of lived experience, or the "prose of the world" (Merleau-Ponty, 1973). Thick description contextualizes experience. It contains the necessary ingredients for thick interpretation, the topic of the next chapter.

A thick description, as discussed in Chapter 1, does more than record what a person is doing. It goes beyond mere fact and surface appearances. It presents detail, context, emotion, and the webs of social relationships that join persons to one another. Thick description evokes emotionality and self-feelings. It inserts history into experience. It establishes the significance of an experience, or the sequence of events, for the person or persons in question. In thick description, the voices, feelings, actions, and meanings of interacting individuals are heard.

Validity and Verisimilitude

A thick description creates verisimilitude; that is, truthlike statements that produce for readers the feeling that they have experienced, or could experience, the events being described. Thick descriptions are valid experiential statements, if by valid, or validity, is meant the ability to produce accounts that are sound, and adequate, and able to be confirmed and substantiated.

There are several different types of thick description. In this chapter these types will be examined, and compared to the different forms of thin description. I shall take up in order the following topics: (1) exemplars of thick description; (2) types and examples of thin description; (3) types of thick description; (4) good and bad thick description; and (5) the relation between description and interpretation.

EXAMPLES OF THICK DESCRIPTION

Thick description may be defined, in part, by its contrast to thin description. Ryle provides an example of thin description:

> You hear someone come out with "Today is the third of February." What is he doing? Obviously the thinnest possible description of what he was doing would fit a gramophone equally well, that he was launching this sequence of syllables into the air [Ryle, 1968, pp. 8-9].

This is a thin description of a person making a statement. It lacks detail and density. Numerous examples of thick description have been given in earlier chapters. (Recall Raskolnikov's crime.) Consider the following, however.

Exemplars: Torture as a Public Spectacle

Foucault (1979, p. 3) opens his book *Discipline and Punish: The Birth of the Prison* with the following thick description of a public torture.

> On 2 March 1757 Damiens the regicide [king] was condemned "to make the *amende honorable* before the main door of the Church of Paris", where he was to be taken and conveyed in a cart, wearing nothing but a shirt, holding a torch of burning wax weighing two pounds . . . where, on a scaffold . . . the flesh will be torn from his breasts, arms, thighs and calves with red-hot pincers . . . then his body drawn and quartered by four horses and his limbs and body consumed by fire, reduced to ashes and his ashes thrown to the winds.

An officer of the watch left this account of the event:

> The executioner, his sleeves rolled up, took the steel pincers . . . and pulled first at the calf of the right leg, then at the thigh . . . then at the breasts . . . Damiens . . . cried out . . . "Pardon, Lord" [Foucault, 1979, 4].

This is a thick description that re-creates a historical situation, the public torture and execution of a king (regicide). It goes beyond a thin account of the execution, which might have simply stated that on the second of March 1757 Damiens, the King of France was executed. (Foucault's presentation of this case goes on for several pages.)

Ways of the Hand

Sociologist David Sudnow (1978, pp. 9-10) is describing the movement of his hands across the piano keyboard as he learns how to play jazz music:

> Sitting at the piano and moving into the production of a chord, the chord as a whole was prepared for as the hand moved toward the keyboard, and the terrain was seen as a field relative to the task. . . .
>
> There was chord A and chord B, separated from one another. . . . A's production entailed a tightly compressed hand, and B's . . . an open and extended spread. . . . The beginner gets from A to B disjointedly.

This is a micro description of the movements of the hand attempting to find proper places on the piano keyboard. A thin description might have stated: "I had trouble learning the piano keyboard." In the next excerpt, Sudnow (1978, p. 30) describes himself some months later playing before a group of friends.

> The Music was not mine. It was going on all around me. I was in the midst of the music. . . . I was up there trying to do this jazz I practiced nearly all day. . . . I was on a bucking bronco of my body's doings . . . between the chord-changing beating of the left hand at more or less regular intervals according to the chart, the melody movements of the right, and the rather more smoothly managed and securely pulsing background of the bass player and drummer, there obtained the most mutually alienative relations.

In this statement, Sudnow is interpreting as he is describing his body's attempts to play jazz music. He is looking down at his own conduct, describing his feelings and his actions at the same time. This description is different from the first, where only actions were depicted.

Running from a Cockfight

Anthropologist Clifford Geertz (1973, pp. 414-15) describes himself and his wife running away from a Balinese cockfight.

> A truck full of policemen armed with machine guns roared up. Amid great screeching cries of "pulisi! pulisi!" from the crowd, the policeman jumped out. . . . People raced down the road, disappeared headfirst over walls . . . my wife and I decided . . . that the thing to do was run too. We ran down the main village street. . . . About halfway down another fugitive ducked suddenly into a compound—his own . . .—and we . . . followed him . . . his wife, who had . . . been through this sort of thing before, whipped out a table, a tablecloth, three chairs, and three cups of tea, and we all . . . sat down . . . and sought to compose ourselves.

Geertz, like Sudnow in the second example, interprets as he describes. A thin description would have stated, "My wife and I ran when the police came, we ended up having tea with a native couple."

THIN DESCRIPTION

I turn next to the characteristics of thin description. As the Ryle quote excerpted above indicates, thin descriptions simply report facts or occurrences. But more is involved.

Characteristics of Thin Description

Elsewhere (Denzin, 1982a, p. 21), I have argued that thin descriptions and interpretations abound in the social sciences. They find their expression in correlation coefficients, path diagrams, F-ratios, dummy variables, structural equations, statistical tests of significance, and social indicators. They are also present in certain forms of qualitative research where the investigator slights description in the rush to formulate interpretations. Indeed, a great deal of interpretive theory in the social sciences is based on thinly described materials. The result has been too much theory and not enough description. David Sudnow's

(1979) study of his piano-playing experiences, as he learned how to improvise at the keyboard, represents the kind of careful mixture and balance of thick description (and thick interpretation) I am advocating.

Thin Descriptions and Types of Words

Thin descriptions gloss, or give superficial, partial, and sparse accounts of, events. They use a few words to describe complex, meaningful events. In this sense, they let big words, often social science terms and concepts, do the work of many little words. Thin descriptions do not present lived experience.

In thin description, the researcher often uses second-order, experience-distant, social science words, instead of first-order, experience-near concepts and terms (Schutz, 1964; Geertz, 1983, pp. 57-58). An experience-near concept is one that "someone—a patient, a subject—in our case an informant—might . . . naturally . . . use to define what he or his fellows see, feel, think, imagine, and so on" (Geertz, 1983, p. 57). An experience-distant concept "is one that specialists . . . an experimenter, an ethnographer . . . employ to forward their scientific . . . aims. . . . Love is an experience-near concept," 'object cathexis' is an experience-distant one (Geertz, 1983, p. 57). Experience-near concepts come from everyday language. Experience-distant concepts come from social science theories. Thin descriptions use experience-distant concepts. Thick descriptions employ experience-near concepts.

Types of Thin Description

There are four basic types of thin descriptions. The first refers to the descriptions given by non-social scientists.

Everyday Glosses

Everyday interactants often gloss, or give only partial accounts of, their actions and experiences (Garfinkel, 1967, pp. 4-5, 20-21). These glossed descriptions permit individuals "to conduct their conversational affairs without interference" (Garfinkel, 1967, p. 42).

Garfinkel (1967, p. 44) offers an example:

My friend and I were talking about a man whose overbearing attitude annoyed us. My friend expressed his feeling.

(S)   I'm sick of him.
(E)   Would you explain what is wrong with you that you are sick?
(S)   Are you kidding? You know what I mean.
(E)   Please explain your ailment.
(S)   (He listened to me with a puzzled look.) What came over you? We
       never talk this way, do we?

When persons are challenged about the meanings of glossed words (i.e.,
"I'm sick of him"), they act with alarm, for they assume that others know
what they mean by their talk.

It is appropriate to collect these kinds of accounts in interpretive
studies because they express how ordinary people describe their
experiences. The interpreter must go deeper, however, and ask that
persons fill in these glosses with actual accounts of experiences and
meanings that give substance to the glossed statement. Interviewers can
probe and attempt to get persons to express the meanings embedded in
their glossed descriptions. If glosses are not filled in, the researcher is left
with surface expressions of meaningful events.

Social Science Glosses

The next three types of thin description refer to the work of social
scientists. The first occurs in those situations where the researcher
slights description in order to give a thick, detailed, theoretical account
of an event or process. The second occurs when the investigator has
collected thick descriptions, but compresses those materials into
summary statements, often using social theory words. In both cases,
experience-distant, second-order terms are used. The third occurs when
the author offers a typified thick description, describing an ideal case,
but not actual experience. The result is thinly described experience. The
next two examples fit the first type of thin description.

Exemplars: Courtship Violence—
Thick Theory, Thin Description

Randall Collins (1975, p. 251) is describing (and interpreting) the
dating system as it works in American youth culture. Force and violence
(rape) are basic features of this system:

A mild use of force is taken into account in the dating system; women
generally allow themselves to be made subject to force only after a tentative

bargain has been struck.... The dating system developed ... just preceding World War I. ... By 1937 Willard Waller had given his analysis of the "rating and dating complex as a system in which marriageable young men and women tried to make erotic conquests and at the same time sorted themselves out into ranks of desirability ... culminating in marriage."

This lengthy statement glosses and compresses, through the use of terms like "rating and dating complex," significant social experiences. These experiences include rape and violence as part of dating and becoming married. There is no lived experience in this description of the American dating system.

Interaction in Small Groups

In a dense theoretical treatment of the emergence of social structure in the small groups laboratory, Couch (forthcoming, pp. 22-23) offers the following thin descriptions:

In all groups when a conflict emerged over the assessment to be made of the intergroup negotiations, the representative attempted to make a more favorable assessment than the constituents. . . . In a few instances conflicting assessments were left dangling. . . . In some groups the representatives and constituents became alienated from each other ... a few groups became . . . hostile to the opposition.

Couch is describing a complex web of group negotiations and inter-actions. Conflict, alienation, and hostility are everywhere present. But he does not describe conflict or hostility, or alienation. He names them. Social science words do the work of description. He glosses what is happening in the groups he is studying.

Medical Work: Glossed Thick Descriptions

In the following example, the researcher glosses a thick description. Strauss (1987, pp. 51-52) offers the following excerpt from an interview with two parents whose young child was born with a congenital heart condition. They had installed a sensitive, high-frequency intercom in the baby's room. They had been told by the doctors to watch their baby at all times.

We did what we had to do ... no other choice. ... The doctors told us to watch her and *not let her get excited.* ... They told us to *look for reactions,*

so the only way that we could do that was to stay up with her. . . . We were
afraid that she would die and we would be asleep. We took turns sleeping
and then sitting with her. This lasted for two months [Strauss, 1987, p. 52,
emphasis in original].

Strauss (1987, p. 53) then comments on this statement by the baby's
mother. He applies a set of distinctions to the parents' activity. This is his
interpretation of their experience:

First-order assessment. Parents do their own assessing, evaluate the
situation based on their awareness of the child's condition. Partial,
sometimes, half-time, all the time—When does the monitoring take place?
How do they know what to monitor?

Here the analyst interprets a thick description and incorporates the
description into a set of theoretical questions that take precedence over
the description. The actual experience is then thinly described. This is
glossed thick description.

Typified Thick Descriptions: Response Cries

In the next example, the researcher acts like he has thick description
when in fact he doesn't. Goffman (1981, pp. 88-89) describes a man
walking down the street:

His general dress and manner have given anyone who views him evidence
of his sobriety, innocent intent, suitable aliveness to the situation. . . . His
left foot strikes an obtruding piece of pavement and he stumbles. He
instantly catches himself, rights himself more or less efficiently, and
continues on.

Up to this point his competence at walking had been taken for granted. . . .
His tripping casts these imputations . . . into doubt. Therefore, before he
continues he may well engage in some actions that have nothing to do with
laws of mechanics.

These actions, which Goffman calls "response cries," may include the
subject saying things like, "*what in the world*!" (Goffman, 1981, p. 90)
and "*hell* or *shit*" (Goffman, 1981, p. 97, emphasis in original). This is
not a real man. He is an ideal type who is used for Goffman's theoretical
purposes. Actual experiences are not described, although many readers

could relate to the experience Goffman has depicted. A typified, thinly veiled thick description is not actual thick description. I turn now to a discussion of the different forms of thick description.

TYPES OF THICK DESCRIPTION

Social scientists have produced several different types of thick description. There are those who describe micro actions, like Sudnow playing the piano. Others describe situations of interaction, like running from a cockfight. Some are historically specific and depict life in an earlier age. Still others describe individuals, or persons in situations, and some depict social relationships. The descriptions that are offered may be incomplete (to be discussed below), complete, glossed (see above), or intrusive; the researchers' interpretations intrude into the description. Finally, there are those descriptions that interpret as they describe: that is, interpretations are part of the description (i.e., Sudnow's account of his playing piano in front of his friends). A discussion of each of these types of thick description is necessary. What passes as thick description is often something else.

A Classification of Types

A full, or complete, thick description is biographical, historical, situational, relational, and interactional. But not every thick description is full or complete. Some focus on relationships, others on individuals, some on situations, and so on. Accordingly, it is possible to classify thick descriptions in terms of on which of the above dimensions they primarily focus. I identify the following types: (1) micro, (2) macro historical, (3) biographical, (4) situational, (5) relational, (6) interactional, (7) intrusive, (8) incomplete, (9) glossed, (10) purely descriptive, and (11) descriptive and interpretive. I will discuss each of these types.

Micro Description

A micro thick description takes a small slice of interaction, experience, or action and records its occurrence in thick detail. It often lacks interpretation. It just describes. Here is an another example from Sudnow (1979, p. 31):

In order to get to the next starting place, I would end it a bit sooner, to give myself time to relocate, feeling the upcoming chord as an encroaching presence whose necessity was fixed by an adherence to the chord chart of the song we were after all "playing together."

Sudnow locates himself within the action he is describing. This is how a micro description is given.

Macro Historical

A macro-historical description attempts to bring an earlier historical moment of experience alive in vivid detail. Foucault's presentation of the public execution of the King of France illustrates a macro-historical, thick description. The account reveals how micro actions shape and in fact constitute major historical events, that is, tearing Damiens's body apart with steel pincers.

Biographical

A biographically thick description focuses on an individual, or a relationship, typically in a situation. In the following excerpt, William Faulkner (1957, p. 5) describes Will Varner, a key figure in his Snopes Family trilogy:

Will Varner, the present owner of the Old Frenchman place, was the chief man of the county. He was the largest landholder and best supervisor in one county and Justice of the Peace in the next and election commissioner in both, and hence the fountainhead if not of law at least of advice and suggestion to the countryside. . . . He was a farmer, a usurer, a veterinarian. . . . He was thin as a fence rail and almost as long, with reddish-gray hair and moustaches and little hard bright innocently blue eyes. . . . He was shrewd secret and merry, of a Rabelaisian turn of mind and very probably still sexually lusty (he had fathered sixteen children to his wife . . .).

In this statement, Faulkner locates Will Varner within a social structure (the county), describes what he does, depicts his physical features, and gives him a brief family history. Biographically thick descriptions often connect individuals to situations, as in the next example.

Biographical Situation

As Gregor Samsa awoke one morning from uneasy dreams he found himself transformed in his hard bed into a gigantic insect. He was lying on his hard, as it were armor-plated, back and when he lifted his head a little he could see his dome-like brown belly divided into stiff arched segments on top of which the bed quilt could hardly keep in position and was about to slide off completely. His numerous legs, which were pitifully thin compared to the rest of his bulk, waved helplessly before his eyes [Kafka, 1952, p. 19].

This description, a frightening account of the metamorphosis of a human body into an insect, creates a picture of Gregor Samsa for the reader. Kafka succeeds (in my opinion) in describing what it would feel like to awake and see one's body in the shape of an insect.

Biographical, situational thick descriptions re-create the sights, sounds, and feelings of persons and places. They permit entry into the situations of experience. They present these situations and biographies in terms of the point of view of the persons being described.

Situational

Thick descriptions of situations read like the following; Jules Henry (1965) is reporting on his impressions of life in a nursing home:

Her room was neat and clean, and the walls were bright yellow. The dresser appeared to one that ought to belong to the patient, and on it were photographs, toiletries, and a heart-shaped box of candy. The patient's hair was curled and combed and had a ribbon in it. She wore powder, rouge and lipstick [Henry, 1965, p. 444].

This description of a situation locates a person in it. It depicts objects in the room, locates them with other objects, and describes the color of the walls and the appearance of the room. The next description is purely situational.

The main hall is wider than the two wings and much more attractive. Walls are a pleasing yellow, the ceilings white . . . the floor is tiled with a grey and black pattern bordered with black . . . the hall is lined on both sides with chairs and there are divans near the east and west ends. . . . The most comfortable chairs are grouped around a small table. . . . An antique umbrella stand is against one wall, and in an alcove . . . is a religious statue on a marble pedestal. The thumb has been broken off and glued back in place. Birds and flower scenes embroidered on Japanese silk framed in bamboo decorate the walls [Henry, 1965, p. 445].

This is a fine-grained description of the main hall in a nursing home. Henry creates a visual picture of the situation.

Relational

A thick relational description brings a relationship alive. Couch's study, discussed above, shows how triads interact in the laboratory. The following statements (Vaughan, 1986, p. 94) describe how intimate and marital partners acted after their lovers or spouses stated that they wanted a divorce or an end to the relationship.

> She began throwing all my books out the window. Obviously it wasn't the books she was throwing out [Student, age 22, separated after living together 2 years].
>
> He and a friend did a midnight raid on the apartment. He destroyed the furniture and stuff that we had gotten since we'd been together [Floral designer, age 28, separated after living together 4 years].
>
> She slashed the tires on my car. She knew that would get me. She even told me she was going to do it [Salesman, age 30, divorced after 3 years].
>
> He put a knife through my face in our wedding picture [Clinical psychologist, age 36, divorced after 8 years].

These accounts vividly describe actions that symbolize the end of relationships. The next statement locates a relational ending in a situation (Vaughan, 1986, p. 157):

> Everybody was home from school . . . the doorbell rang so the kids answered the door and I was browning the veal and they're saying, "Mom, come to the door. Somebody wants ya." And I said, "But I can't. You tell 'em," you know. They said, "No mom, they said they have to see you." I went to the door and the sheriff handed me a subpoena for a divorce. And the kids are saying, "Mom, what is it?" And they're all standing around me. Here I am with the kids standing around me. "Daddy wants a divorce?" And I started to cry. So, I mean everything is burned and we all sat in here.

This thick description re-creates a slice of interactional experience. It contains dialogue and interaction. It takes the reader into the situation and tells how this woman received the information concerning her husband's desire for a divorce. It connects a turning point experience to its moment of occurrence.

Interactional

Interactional thick descriptions, like the example just given, focus on interactions between two or more persons. Here is a man describing how he beat up his wife.

> I come home tired and beat. The house was a mess, the dogs were loose, and she was in the bedroom taking a nap. Supper wasn't even started yet. I fixed a drink, turned on the news. She came out, yelled at me for having that drink. I'd heard it a thousand times before. I couldn't take it anymore. I threw the drink in her face, grabbed her arm and yelled, "Where's my God-Damned supper! You never do anything around here." She hit back at me, called me no good. She ran and got my wood carving that I'd been making her for Christmas. She laughed at it, called it stupid and dumb. She threw it against the wall. That's when I lost it. I ran at her. She called the police [Denzin, 1984b, p. 501].

This statement combines three features of a thick description. It is interactional, situational, and relational. It contains some glosses ("I'd heard it a thousand times before," "That's when I lost it"), but it is primarily descriptive. It re-creates, in the man's words, the fight that he had with his wife.

Intrusive Descriptive

In an intrusive description, the researcher's interpretations enter into and shape the description as it is reported. When this occurs, it is difficult to capture the "native's point of view" (Geertz, 1983, pp. 55-69). His or her perspective is seen through the researcher's eyes.

Here is an intrusive description. Geertz (1973, pp. 420-421) is discussing the moral and symbolic significance of the cockfight in Bali:

> In the cockfight, man and beast, good and evil, ego and id, the creative power or aroused masculinity, and the destructive power of loosened animalilty fuse in a bloody drama of hatred, cruelty, violence and death.

In the next passage, Geertz (1973, p. 422) describes the cockfight:

> Most of the time, in any case, the cocks fly almost immediately at one
> another in a wing-beating, head-thrusting, leg-kicking explosion of
> animal fury, so absolute, and in its own way so beautiful, as to be almost
> abstract, a Platonic concept of hate.

In these lines, Geertz departs both from pure description and from that
form of description that incorporates the native's interpretations into
the text (see below, Chapter 6, and Crapanzano, 1986, pp. 68-76).

In the first excerpt, he attributes all sorts of experiences and
motivations to the Balinese, likening their cockfight to the play between
Freud's id and ego, and to the aroused forces of destructive animality
(see Crapanzano, 1986, p. 72). In the second excerpt, the fight itself, he
discusses the actions of the cocks in terms of the Platonic concept of
hate, and sees in the fight a beautiful animal fury that is pure and
absolute. These are his interpretations. These are not the words of a Bali
cockfighter. These interpretations intrude into his descriptions of the
fight. As a result, the reader does not know what a Bali cockfight looks
or feels like. The native's point of view is lost. The reader is asked to see
the fight as Geertz does. But lacking a description of the fight, the reader
is only left with Geertz's words.

Incomplete

The incomplete thick description begins to present events or experiences in a thick fashion, but at some point interrupts itself and
summarizes, or glosses, significant information. In the following
excerpt, Isabelle Bertaux-Wiame (1981, p. 261) reports an interview
with a young French woman who had left her small village and moved to
Paris at the age of 20.

> I was in a bakery—my employers were very nice, but there was only me to
> deliver the bread to the farms around, with the horse van. It was hard
> work. And then, one day, it was getting late, it was almost dark, there was
> a corner in the road, and the horse took fright and bolted. I was that
> frightened that the very next day, I left the job. I decided to come to Paris
> to look up an old childhood friend, whose parents had a hotel. I sent word
> to her and without even waiting for a reply, I set out.

In this statement, the young woman explains her going to Paris in terms
of the frightening experience with the horse. This is a thick description

that is biographical, historical, and interactional. It gives an account for a turning point moment in this woman's life.

Consider the following lines in Bertaux-Wiame's (1981, p. 261) text, however:

> It was only later on that she [the young woman] mentioned in a whisper that she had had a fiance, but the engagement had been broken off: I had to go, I had known a young man.

It was not the experience with the horse that led her to move to Paris. It was her sexual relationship with her fiancé. Bertaux-Wiame (1981, p. 262) offers a dense theoretical interpretation of the "marriage market" in small French villages and its pressures on young women to marry fiancés with whom they have had sex. When her engagement broke off, the woman was no longer marriageable under the rules of the village. She was not a virgin. She could have stayed in the village and lived the life of a spinster, "letting her fault determine her whole life" (Bertaux-Wiame, 1981, p. 262).

The problem with an incomplete thick description is that it glosses the actual experiences that shape what is being described and interpreted. Bertaux-Wiame does not give the reader access to the thoughts and words of this young girl. She lets her interpretations do the work of actual description. In this respect, an incomplete description is like its intrusive counterpart.

Glossed

A glossed thick description has been discussed above, in terms of thin descriptions that purport to be thick. The last excerpt from Geertz's description of the cockfight in Bali is glossed.

Purely Descriptive

Strictly speaking, there can be no pure description. The words that are used to describe a phenomenon or experience create what is described. I use the word "pure" to reference the relative absence of intrusive interpretations in the description. Here is an example.

> That early morning, in January 1933, only one person was awake on the street . . . call him Samuel Bennet. He wore a trilby hat that had been lying

by his bedside. . . . In striped pajamas tight under his arms and torn
between the legs, he padded barefoot downstairs and opened the
breakfast-room door of his parents' six-room house [Thomas, 1964, p. 3].

This is how Samuel Bennet started his morning. In a few minutes, he
would destroy family photographs and china as he left his home for good,
to make his way as an adult in the outside world. This description offers
no intrusive interpretation. Like Sudnow's account of his early days of
piano playing, it just describes.

Descriptive and Interpretive

The descriptive and interpretive thick description records interpretations that occur within the experience as it is lived. Sudnow's account of
how he felt as he played before friends is both descriptive and
interpretive. These types of statements are difficult to produce and
obtain. They require a person who is able to reflect on experience as it
occurs. Such accounts are invaluable, however, because they show how
interpretations shape interaction and experience. Here is Sudnow (1978,
p. 152) again:

From an upright posture I look down at my hands on the piano keyboard
during play, with a look that is hardly a look at all. But standing back I
find that I proceed through and in a terrain nexus, doing singings with my
fingers, so to speak, a single voice at the tips of my fingers, going for each
next note in sayings just now and just then . . . I sing with my fingers, so to
speak.

Summary

Table 5.1 summarizes this rather lengthy discussion of the types and
forms of thick description. It lists each form, and indicates its relative
emphasis on the biographical, situational, relational, and interactional
dimensions of a thick description.

I have divided this table into three sections.[1] Types 1-6 describe the
focus of the description: micro, macro, biography, situational, relational, and interactional. Types 7-9 reflect interpretations of descriptions, that is, whether they are intrusive, incomplete, or glossed. Types
10-11 focus solely on description, or on a mix of description and
interpretation. Types 7-9 are to be avoided.

TABLE 5.1
Types of Thick Description

Form	Biography	Historical	Situational	Relational	Interactional
1. Micro	seldom	possible	yes	yes	yes
2. Macro	possible	yes	possible	possible	yes
3. Biography	always	yes	yes	possible	yes
4. Situational	possible	yes	always	possible	possible
5. Relational	possible	yes	possible	always	yes
6. Interaction	seldom	possible	yes	yes	always
7. Intrusive	yes	yes	yes	yes	yes
8. Incomplete	yes	yes	yes	yes	yes
9. Glossed	yes	yes	yes	yes	yes
10. Pure Descriptive	yes	yes	yes	yes	yes
11. Descriptive-Interpretive	yes	yes	yes	yes	yes

NOTE: yes = content and focus will be present (for forms 7-11, the effect of the focus can be positive or negative); no = content and focus will be absent; possible = content and focus can be present.

A further examination of this table indicates that some forms are more likely to have an emphasis on one dimension than another, that is, biography versus history, and so on. A fully triangulated study would contain thick descriptions that encompass each form and content, or focus dimension.

GOOD AND BAD THICK DESCRIPTION

A good thick description is not glossed, intrusive, or incomplete. A bad description will gloss details, insert the observer's interpretations into the flow of experience that is being recorded, and will omit, or give only slight descriptive attention to, key details. I have given numerous examples of what I regard as good, thick description.

Learning to Listen and Writing Bad Thick Description

In Chapter 6, I will present an interpretation of the following excerpts from my fieldwork on A.A. I offer them here as an example of bad thick description.

In the last chapter, I argued that the individual who becomes a member of A.A. learns how to listen to what is said around the A.A. tables. He or she learns the meanings of new words. The member learns to listen. The interpretive researcher must do the same thing. How is this done? The following example from my field notes, taken after I had visited five A.A. meetings, reveals how it is *not* done. I entitled these notes "The Structure of an A.A. Meeting." This is what I wrote to myself.

"The Structure of an A. A. Meeting"

1. Opening, Welcome.
2. Serenity Prayer—a moment of silence.
3. "How It Works" (read by one person, all listen in silence).
4. The 12 Traditions (read by one person, all listen in silence).
5. Any new members?—introduced by first name (or newcomers).
6. Announcements—can be made by any member, usually of a new meeting, social announcements, etc.
7. If a new member, the First Step (by tradition with a new member discuss the First Step).
8. In turn each person speaks on the First Step, with the new person given an opportunity to speak, if he or she chooses.
9. If no new member, a topic for discussion is given, may come from the *BIG BOOK,* the thought for the day, any problem dealing with the program— time, the past, responsibility, growing, guilt, tolerance for others.
10. The donation (this is usually made during the readings, but can come anytime in the meeting, depending on the meeting, number of persons present, etc.).
11. The closing—"Does anyone else have anything else they would like to add? If not, we will close in the usual manner." (The Lord's Prayer, all hold hands, speak together, and end with "Keep on Coming Back").
12. Members depart, break up and leave the table, chat in small gatherings, empty ashtrays, gather up coffee cups, rearrange chairs, etc.

This is flawed, thick description. It is intrusive, glossed, and incomplete. My words are all over the place. The voices of A.A. members are nowhere present. I acted "as if" I understood how a meeting worked. I made no mention of biographies, histories, relationships, or interactions. I presented a purely structural picture of a meeting. An inspection of these materials reveals where work needs to be done; that is, precisely on the points just listed. Bad thick description can be put to good use, but only if one has sense enough to stay in the field long enough to learn what he or she doesn't know. In the next section, I take up the problem of the relationship between description and interpretation.

DESCRIPTION AND INTERPRETATION

In thick description, the researcher attempts to rescue and secure the meanings, actions, and feelings that are present in an interactional experience (but see Geertz, 1973, p. 20). Description is necessarily interpretive, as I have shown above. It captures the interpretations persons bring to the events that have been captured. It records the interpretations that are made by interactants as interaction unfolds. It provides the grounds for the researcher's (and the reader's) interpretations of the events and meanings that have been captured. The words that record description are also interpretive.

Thick description involves capturing, and if possible determining, the meanings a particular action or sequence of actions has for the individuals in question. The capturing of meaningful events is done through the triangulated use of the several methods of recording and capturing life experiences discussed in Chapters 1, 2, and 3 (personal experience stories, self-stories, collecting slices of interaction, interviews). Thick description is biographical and interactional. It connects self-stories and personal histories to specific interactional experiences.

Thick description creates the conditions for thick interpretation, which is the topic of the next chapter. Thick interpretation gives meaning to the descriptions and interpretations given in the events that have been recorded. A good interpretation is one that "takes us to the heart of what is being interpreted" (Geertz, 1973, p. 18). Thick interpretation attempts to uncover the "conceptual structures that inform our subject's acts" (Geertz, 1973, p. 27).

Levels of Meaning

Thick interpretation constructs a system of analysis and understanding that is meaningful within the worlds of lived experience. It assumes that any experience has meaning at two levels: the surface (or the intended) and the deep (unintended) (Freud, 1900 [1965]). Meaning, which must be captured in interpretation, is symbolic. It moves in surface and deep directions at the same time. Thick interpretation attempts to unravel and record these multiple meaning structures that flow from interactional experience. It assumes that multiple meanings will always be present in any situation. No experience ever has the same meaning for two individuals. This is so because meaning is emotional and biographical.

Summarizing the discussion, thick description has the following characteristics:

(1) It builds on multiple, triangulated, biographical methods.
(2) It connects biography to lived experience.
(3) It is contextual, historical, and interactional.
(4) It captures the actual flow of experience of individuals and collectivities in a social situation.
(5) It captures the meanings that are present in a sequence of experience.
(6) It allows the reader to experience vicariously the essential features of the experiences that have been described and are being interpreted.
(7) It attempts not to gloss what is being described.

Thick interpretation has the following characteristics (which will be developed in the next chapter):

(1) It rests upon and interprets thick descriptions.
(2) It assumes that meaning is symbolic and operates at the surface and deep levels.
(3) It attempts to unravel the multiple meanings that are present in any interactional experience.
(4) It has the objective of constructing an interpretation that is meaningful to the persons studied.

Thick interpretation attempts to conform to the criteria of interpretation discussed in Chapters 2 and 3.

CONCLUSIONS

In this chapter, I have offered an extended discussion of thick and thin descriptions. A typology of each type of description was offered. Research illustrations were taken from the actual descriptive work of sociologists and anthropologists and, in a few cases, novelists (Faulkner and Kafka). These research examples indicate that what passes as description is often something else; namely, interpretation. Criteria for evaluating descriptions were given. In the next chapter, I will take up the complex problems involved in interpreting descriptions.

NOTE

1. David R. Maines and Debra J. Rog helped clarify these divisions for me.

6

Doing Interpretation

In this chapter, types of interpretation are treated. Interpretation is understood to refer to the attempt to explain the meaning of a term. An interpreter translates the unfamiliar into the familiar. The act of interpreting gives meaning to an experience. Meaning refers to that which is in the mind or the thoughts of a person. Meaning, in this sense, speaks to the signification, purpose, and consequences of a set of experiences for an individual. Meaning is embedded in the stories persons tell about their experiences. Once experiences have been interpreted, understandings of them can be understood. In understanding, the meaning of an experience is comprehended and grasped. Understandings can be emotional and cognitive. I will offer exemplars of thick and thin interpretation. The relationship between description, interpretation, and understanding will be discussed.

Mindful of the meanings of the above terms, interpretive interactionists interpret and render understandable turning point moments of experience, or the epiphanies, in the lives of ordinary individuals. They interpret these moments as they have been thickly described. These interpretations make understanding possible. It is not enough to just describe. Interpretations and understandings must be produced and conveyed to the reader. In the last chapter, the various forms of thick description were discussed.

In this chapter, I will discuss how interpretation is done. I will treat the following issues: (1) exemplars of interpretation, (2) the interpretation of interpretations, (3) what interpretation does and what is interpreted, (4) types of interpretation, and (5) the relationship between description and interpretation (once again) and understanding.

The framework developed in the last chapter for analyzing types of thick description will be employed in this chapter. I will treat micro, macro, biographical, situational, relational, interactional, intrusive, incomplete, and glossed interpretations. I will also maintain the distinction, briefly discussed in the last chapter, between native interpretations and observer interpretations. This will lead to a discussion of the differences between native and social science theories of the experience.

The Importance of Interpretation and Understanding

I argued in Chapter 1 that interpretive studies need a focus. The project I've chosen examines the existentially problematic, emotional experiences that occur in the lives of ordinary people. These are experiences that make a difference. They connect personal troubles to public issues and to applied programs that address such problems. For example, hot lines for battered women and alcoholism treatment centers for alcoholics. By studying and interpreting these experiences, researchers can hope to comprehend and understand better the personal trouble of individuals in the late postmodern period. With such understandings comes knowledge that can be used to help such persons more effectively. This knowledge can also be used to evaluate programs that have been implemented to assist troubled persons. *The perspectives and experiences of those persons who are served by applied programs must be grasped, interpreted, and understood if solid, effective, applied programs are to be put into place.* This argument organizes this chapter.

EXEMPLARS OF INTERPRETATION

It will be perhaps useful to begin with an example of bad interpretation. Recall my field notes on the "Structure of an A.A. Meeting" discussed at the end of the last chapter. In those notes, I described the major moments in an A.A. meeting. Here are the interpretations I wrote.

The A.A. Meeting

Discussion

1. REFLEXIVITY builds as each discussant often turns back to what another speaker has said, seldom are persons explicitly complimented on personal realities that lie behind statements, although points may be praised or built upon.
2. NAMES—First names only, unless the group is made up of long-standing persons, when on occasion a first name will be attached to a familiar name—e.g., Bill _____ , or Bob _____ . Because many persons have the same first names, elements of personal appearance are added to differentiate speakers, e.g., Ted with the blond hair, etc.
3. PHRASES—"You're only human," "You're in the right place," "One day at a time," "First Things First," "Easy Does It," "I know I can drink again," "The urge has left me," "I pray that it leaves me," "I'm still an alcoholic," "I still have a drink, a binge left in me," "I've come so far," "Being at the tables," "The tables," "The program," "Since I was in

treatment," "The club," "I know I'm talking too much," "Does this make sense?" "I used to be a periodic alcoholic."

4. INTERPRETATION—Each member/speaker interprets the topic for the evening, or the day and does so by referring either to concrete events in his or her life—"My son-in-law broke his neck at work yesterday. If I were still drinking I wouldn't be able to handle it."—or, reference is more abstract, "How well my life has become since I stopped drinking . . ."

5. From these individual interpretations strands of meaning and interpretation of the meeting emerge: "This has been a good meeting." "I'm really glad I came tonight," "This has been very good for me." "Thanks for such a good meeting."

6. Out of these interpretations, which are individual, arises an individual's understanding of their place within the program for that particular meeting and evening. They weave strands of interpretation into their understanding of the program and of their own program and reaffirm their bond to the tables and THE PROGRAM. From this reaffirmation flows an understanding that leaves the tables and flows through the person's relational dealings in the everyday world of significant others. They carry these interpretations and meanings—as residues of constructed and reconstructed experience—out into a drinking world where temptations of drinking and areas of conflict are everywhere.

7. The program works at three levels: (1) admitting and accepting alcoholism; (2) the daily working on the interpersonal problems and character defects that flow from an old personality that drank; (3) daily reminding the person of the rewards of sobriety—how much better things are getting. The meetings and the tables are used to reinforce each of these levels, and as new members come into the program each member can see him or herself in the despair of the person who has fallen or is still drinking [November 2, 1981].

This ends the interpretation.

Interpreting a First Interpretation

These notes reveal several features of the interpretive process. First, they are glosses, or summaries, of experience. They include no knowledge of who the A.A. speakers were. They evince no understanding of the nuances of A.A. language or A.A. history. They evince no understanding of the history of this A.A. group. Nor do they indicate how these rituals and Steps work for the A.A. member. Second, as glosses on experience, they stand as abstractions that record no lived experience. There is no thick description here (see Chapter 5). This is thin description. Third, these notes reveal an arrogance on my part. I assumed that I understood what was going on in an A.A. meeting. In fact, I did not understand what was going on. Fourth, I prejudiced my understandings by focusing only on what occurred at the beginning of the meeting. I thought that what was read was what was most important in the meeting. I would later learn that what is read is important, but not for the reasons that I thought when I took these notes. Fifth, I did not hear what A.A. members said. I assumed that everybody said pretty much the same thing. I assumed that I did not have to listen to what was said by each member. Sixth, I assumed that every A.A. meeting was the same. I later learned that this is not the case.

The interpretations that I offered in my discussion of my notes are also thin and highly speculative. I would later discover that my early understanding of reflexivity in A.A. talk was superficial. A.A. talk is dialogical. It takes as its focus the group and the experiences of the person talking. When an A.A. member talks, he or she speaks to the entire group, not to a specific individual. No one is expected to respond to this dialogue: It is a self-dialogue with the group.

In a similar manner, I later learned that A.A. members do learn each other's last names and that the tags that I identified (Ted with the blond hair) were the tags that newcomers use. Within any A.A. meeting, one or more members will know the biography that stands behind a first name, including (often) the person's last name. The phrases that I recorded ("One Day At a Time" and so on) are part of A.A. talk in any A.A. meeting. They reflect how the speakers have located themselves within A.A. folklore and appropriated that folklore to their self-stories. I would later learn that members can be identified by the segment of A.A. folklore they characteristically use when they talk. I did not know this when I wrote these notes and interpretations.

My interpretations of the talk I had heard at meetings failed to grasp how a member weaves talking into his or her personal life. I failed to see that an essential part of A.A. talk is being able to locate an experience in one's life that could be a reason for drinking and then showing how one in fact did not drink. I failed to grasp the single-minded goal of the A.A. member, which is to stay sober at any cost. My statements under point seven hinted at this understanding, but failed to grasp its significance for the A.A. member. These notes reveal how a researcher who does not know how to listen takes field notes and makes interpretations.

Taking Time

Interpretation is a temporal process. By this I mean the following. First, it takes time to learn the language of the group that is being studied. Second, as argued in Chapter 4, the biographies of the persons who speak the language must be learned. This knowledge takes the researcher farther into the social structure of the group being studied. It shows how each individual's life experiences shape how they talk, use the language, and tell stories. Third, the relationships that exist between the persons in the group must be learned. Fourth, the interpreter must be able to call out in him- or herself the range of meanings that any word, phrase, or term, has for a group member. This process of taking the attitude of the other (Mead, 1934) is a linguistic and emotional process. It can only occur after the researcher has become immersed in the group. The researcher, to repeat a point made earlier, must be able to live him-or herself into the life experiences of the group. If this is not done, superficial, thin interpretations will be written.

It took three years before I felt comfortable with the A.A. language and the meaning structures that lie behind that language. Because interpretation is a temporal process, researchers are advised to study those areas of social life where they have some intimate familiarity. By doing so, he or she can draw upon the stock of knowledge that has been built up out of previous life experiences. This is one of the consequences of C. W. Mills's directive to connect personal biography with socio-logical inquiry.

WHAT INTERPRETATION DOES

Interpretation builds, as noted earlier, on description. It gives meaning to experiences that have been thickly described. Interpretation makes sense out of expressions of experience. The experience that is made sense of is expressed symbolically (see below). These symbolic expressions often take the form of personal experience and self-stories. In some instances, meaningful experience may be expressed drama-tically, in the form of performed texts or performances (Bruner, 1986, p. 7; Turner, 1986). Interpretive interactionists interpret these symbolic and interactional expressions of meaningful, turning point experiences.

Types of Interpreters

Interpretation is done by an interpreter. There are two types of interpreters: the people who have actually experienced what has been described, and so called well-informed experts, who are often ethnographers, sociologists, or anthropologists. These two types of interpreters (local and social science) will often give different meanings to the same set of thickly described experiences. (The differences in these two types of interpretations will be discussed below.)

Interpretation clarifies and untangles the meanings that are produced by a set of experiences. It does so within an interpretive framework that is meaningful to those who have experienced the event in question; that is, interpretation utilizes experience-near concepts and interpretations. An interpretation, as Geertz (1973, p. 27) argues, illuminates the meanings and conceptual structures that organize a subject's experience.

Theories of Interpretation

What does this statement mean? It means that individuals have working theories of their conduct and their experiences. These theories derive from their fellows. They are contained in the oral and printed cultural texts of the group. These theories are based on the "local knowledge" (Geertz, 1983) that individuals and groups have about those experiences that matter to them. These theories are pragmatic, that is, they work (see James, 1955; Peirce, 1934). They work because they give meaning to problematic experiences. These meanings allow persons to deal with the problems that confront them. These theories may be fatalistic, idealistic, religious, spiritual, ideological, political, or fantastic. They may draw from social science theories, or they may be passed on, in an oral tradition, from one generation to another.

An Example

Here is an example of a local theory of interpretation. The speaker has been sober in A.A. for 10 years.

I used to drink every day. Then I came to A.A. and learned that I got a disease called alcoholism. I got sober by coming to meetings, reading the Big Book, working the Steps and getting myself a sponsor. I got a spiritual

Program and I work with newcomers. I haven't had a drink since I started
doing all of these things [Male, 45 years old, divorced, house painter].

Narratives, Stories, and
Local Theories of Interpretation

This man's statement contains an interpretation of why he is sober. It
invokes A.A.'s theory of alcoholism (a disease), and recovery (go to
meetings, read the *Big Book*, work with others, and so on). The theory
says, "If you do these things you will get and stay sober." He did these
things and he has been sober for 10 years. He is pragmatically using
A.A.'s theory to help him deal with a problem in his life. His theory is
A.A.'s theory. In the above account, he has given a glossed statement of
this theory. (Glossed interpretations will be discussed in detail below.)
His statement takes the form of a narrative, or an abbreviated story. It
has a beginning, a middle, and an end. It states that he used to drink
every day, then he started coming to A.A. meetings where he learned
that he had a disease called alcoholism. In A.A. (the middle part of his
narrative), he acquired a spiritual program. The end of his story states
that he hasn't had a drink since he started doing all of these things.

A major goal of interpretation is to uncover these theories, often told
in the form of stories, that structure the experiences of the persons being
studied. Interpretive interactionism assumes, as argued in Chapter 1,
that for certain purposes all one needs to do is uncover these local
theories of interpretation. When this is done, the conceptual structures
that inform a subject's actions will have been uncovered. Unless this is
done, the subject's point of view is ignored. Without this point of view,
evaluations or interpretations of the subject's actions are likely to be
built on theories that are not in tune with actual experiences. When this
occurs, applied research programs risk failure. They will not be in touch
with the people they are intended to serve. There will be occasions,
however, when a subject's theory is incomplete, biased, and self-serving.
When this occurs, the researcher must go beyond the subject's definitions
of experience to other interpretations (see the discussion below).

The seeds of interpretation, then, are always contained within the
experiences that have been thickly described. But these experiences
must be collected and located within a group and its cultural meanings.
The interpreter needs to learn how to see and hear these theories. This is
what interpretation does.

Interpretation Is Symbolic

In the last chapter, I suggested that experience always has at least two levels of meaning, the surface and the deep. What an act means on the surface is perhaps not what it means at a deeper, more symbolic level. An event, because it is experienced and captured within language, is symbolic. This means that interpretation is always symbolic. First, an event or experience can be interpreted in multiple ways. A simple "Hello," spoken abruptly, in anger, does not carry the same meaning as a "Hello" spoken with a smile, accompanied by a warm handshake. If interpretation is symbolic, then the multiple meanings that are conveyed by words, phrases, and gestures must be grasped and understood. This means that interpretation must always be contextualized. The word "Hello" has different meanings in different contexts.

Interpretation is symbolic in a second way. The expressions of the meanings of an experience are given in symbolically meaningful ways, often as stories or narratives. These symbolic expressions may extend beyond storytelling practices, to rituals and ritual performances, social dramas, and statements given in the cultural texts of the group (see Bruner, 1986, p. 145; Turner, 1986, p. 41). These symbolic expressions of meaningful experience must be collected and studied (see Rosaldo, 1986). In them, the researcher learns how subjects collectively and individually define themselves in their moments of crisis.

TYPES OF INTERPRETATION AND EXEMPLARS

There are several different types of interpretation that may be written, or secured, by the observer. As noted at the beginning of this chapter, interpretations, like the descriptions they build upon, may be micro, macro, biographical, situational, relational, interactional, intrusive, incomplete, glossed, thick, or thin. Rather than repeat the discussion of these types (see Chapter 5) I will focus on only the following types of interpretation: (1) thin, (2) thick, (3) native, (4) observer, (5) analytic, (6) descriptive-contextual, (7) relational-interactional. A brief discussion of each is required.

Thin interpretation: response cries. A thin interpretation is a gloss. It often offers a causal interpretation of a sequence of action, such as "person A ran across the road because the bus was coming." A thin interpretation, like its counterpart, thin description, does not give detail on context, biography, interaction, history, or social relationships. Here is an example. Recall the discussion of Goffman's man who stumbles while walking along the street (Chapter 5). When this man falters he utters an apology, or account to others, who may have seen him stumble. He engages, Goffman (1981, p. 89) asserts, in the following action:

> Our subject externalizes a presumed inward state and acts so as to make discernible the special circumstances which presumably produced it. He tells a little story in the situation.

In so doing, this man, Goffman argues, breaks the prescriptive rule of communication of *"no talking to oneself in public"* (Goffman, 1981, p. 88, emphasis in original). This is a thin, glossed, analytic interpretation (see below). It lacks context, biography, history, and interaction. It does not rest on thick description.

Thick interpretation: alcoholic slips. Thick interpretation elaborates and builds upon thick description (see the discussion at the end of Chapter 5). A thick interpretation incorporates context, interaction, and history. Consider the following. It is taken from my book *The Recovering Alcoholic* (Denzin, 1987b). I am discussing the slips, or relapses, of alcoholics after they have attended A.A. for a period of time.

> Alcoholics who slip do so only to the extent that they define themselves as "situational alcoholics." Such members come to A.A. out of an attempt to solve a particular problem in their life. When that problem is solved they relinquish the identity of alcoholic and return to previous conceptions of themselves [Denzin, 1987b, p. 151].

When the above process occurs, and if the member confronts a problem over which he or she used to drink, a relapse will occur. The above statement interprets slips in light of context, history, biography, and interaction. It is based on an extensive description of alcoholic identities (Denzin, 1987b, chap. 5).

Native interpretation, contextual-relational: battered wives. A native interpretation, as discussed above, states the meaning of an experience in terms of the local knowledge of the individuals actually involved in the experience. A native interpretation may be thick or thin. Here is an example. Johnson and Ferraro (1984, p. 121) report the following statement from a woman beaten by her alcoholic husband. She explains her decision to leave him after he made a direct threat on her life. It takes the form of a story.

It was like a pendulum. He'd swing to the extremes both ways. He'd get
drunk and beat me up, and then he'd get sober and treat me like a queen.
One day he put a gun to my head and pulled the trigger. It wasn't loaded.
But that's when I decided I'd had it. I sued for separation of property.

This statement contains an interpretation of the woman's actions. She
made the decision to leave when her husband put the gun to her head.
This interpretation is contextual, relational, historical, and interactional.

Observer interpretation. Johnson and Ferraro (1984, p. 121) state, in
regard to this case and others like it, that

women who suddenly realize that their lives are literally in danger may
begin the victimization process. . . . Life itself is more important to
maintain than the relationship.

This interpretation grows out of the woman's interpretations of her
experiences. It makes sense in light of her statement. It is unlike my
earlier interpretation of the A.A. meeting or Geertz's reading (below) of
the Balinese cockfight. These other interpretations impose the observer's
framework on the native's experiences.

Types of Observer Interpretations:
Voices and Dialogue

An observer interpretation may also be thick or thin. It may build
upon local interpretations or it may impose the observer's own
interpretation on the experiences that have been described. An observer
interpretation may be *monologic* and suppress the voices of those
studied. It presents their experiences through the observer's words (see
the examples from Geertz). On the other hand, such interpretations may
be *dialogic* and *polyphonic*: that is, they reflect a dialogue between the
observer and those studied, and they allow many different voices and
interpretations to speak from the writer's text (see Bruner, 1986;
Bakhtin, 1981; Jordan, 1987; and the examples below). Dialogic and
polyphonic interpretations are preferred, because they allow multiple
voices of interpretation to be heard.

Dialogic and polyphonic interpretation: Twelve Stepping. Here is an
example of a dialogic, polyphonic interpretation. It also is taken from my
study of the recovering alcoholic. In the following excerpts, A.A. members
are discussing what "Twelve Stepping" means to them. (In A.A., Twelve
Stepping refers to carrying the A.A. message to a suffering alcoholic.)

Tn: I have a problem. I got a neighbor who is fighting with this thing (alcoholism). Yesterday I went over and I gave it to him straight. I said . . . he needed help.

Ws: I'm Ws. I'm an alcoholic. I wasn't going to speak today. Eight years ago today they took me to the fifth floor . . . for crazies. I was Twelve Stepped while I was there. You had a successful Twelve Step. . . . You came back sober. . . .

Khy: I'm Khy. I'm an alcoholic. I don't know what got me sober. It was many different things. It had to be a sum that was greater than its parts . . .

Dv: I'm Dv. I'm an alcoholic . . . I'm working with someone right now. He's sober . . . then drunk . . . then sober, then drunk. I don't know how it works. I know I was successfully Twelve Stepped [Denzin, 1987b, p. 111].

In this excerpt, four voices speak. Each speaker defines in his or her words the meaning of Twelve Stepping. Tn. speaks about carrying the message to his neighbor. Ws. describes his own experiences while being on a psychiatric ward. Khy. describes her recovery, and Dv. discusses how he is working with an alcoholic who is still drinking. I call this a dialogic, polyphonic, or multivoiced interpretation.

Analytic interpretation. An analytic interpretation imposes an abstract, often causal scheme on a set of events or experiences. It typically derives from a theory the observer has imported into the research situation, although it may be derived from the setting (see Geertz's propositions about the Balinese cockfight and the discussion below).

Descriptive-contextual: making jazz. A descriptive-contextual interpretation is fit to the concrete experiences being interpreted. It is necessarily biographical and historical, ideographic and emic. It is particularizing and interprets a case, or experience, in terms of its unique properties and dimensions. A descriptive-contextual interpretation should be multivoiced (polyphonic) and dialogical, although this may not always be possible, or even necessary. Here is David Sudnow talking about his advancing ability to make jazz music on the piano:

As the time got into the fingers, hands, arms, shoulders, everywhere, altogether new relationships between chords and paths were being fulfilled. . . . I would do jazz sayings that increasingly brought my full "vocabular" resources, my full range of wayful reaching, into the service of the jazz on the records [Sudnow, 1978, p. 141].

In this statement, Sudnow is interpreting his ability to make music like the music on the records. He does this in terms of time; time getting into his fingers, hands, arms, and shoulders. This is a thick, descriptive, contextual, interactional interpretation.

Two types of descriptive interpretation: factual and interpretive. There are two types of descriptive interpretations. The first is factual. A descriptive-contextual interpretation may presume to record a set of experiences objectively. The second type is interpretive. It rests on native narrative accounts of experiences. An objective-descriptive interpretation attempts to work with facts. An interpretive-narrative account presents experiences as they have been interpreted, and makes no pretense about being factually accurate or resting on facts per se (see discussion below, and the discussion of Twelve Stepping above).

Relational-interactional. A relational-interactional interpretation makes sense of a set of experiences in terms of the social relationships and interactions that occur in the situation. *All interpretations should be relational and interactional, as well as contextual* (Couch, 1984). Such interpretations should rest on thick descriptions and be nonanalytic.

There are interrelationships between the above types of interpretation. I turn now to an extended discussion of each.

Thin, Analytic, Observer-Based Interpretations: Geertz and the Balinese Cockfight

In the last chapter, I offered several excerpts from Geertz's study of the cockfight in Bali. I suggested that his descriptions too often blurred interpretations with descriptions. Here is another statement by Geertz (1973, pp. 450-51):

> Enacted and re-enacted, so far without end, the cockfight enables the Balinese, as read and reread, *Macbeth* enables us, to see a dimension of his own subjectivity. . . . In the cockfight, then, the Balinese forms and discovers his temperament and his society's temper at the same time.

What does this statement mean? Geertz is comparing the text of the cockfight to a Shakespeare play, and is suggesting that both texts create subjective understandings for their readers. How does he know this? These are Geertz's interpretations of the cockfight. They are not the meanings a Balinese male or female brings to the occasion of a fight.

Consider the following, more abstract interpretation of the cockfight. Here Geertz (1973, p. 441) states his understandings in terms of propositions.

1. The closer the identification of cock and man . . . the more the man will advance his best . . . cock.

2. The greater the emotion that will be involved and the more the general absorption in the match . . . the "solider" the citizens who will be gaming.

Geertz (1973, p. 441) states that this is a formal paradigm, designed to display the logical "not the causal structure of cockfighting." In these two propositions, he has offered what I call an *analytic interpretation* (see above and the discussion below) of a key cultural text. It contains several problematic terms: "identification," "best cock," "greater the emotion," "general absorption," "solid citizens." The meanings of these terms are not given. These terms and the interpretations Geertz builds with them stand several levels above the actual experience of the cockfight.

His interpretations are decontextual, nonrelational, and noninteractional. They are thinly disguised as thick interpretations. They are monologic and suppress the native's voices. They are not dialogical, for Geertz imposes his interpretations on the native's experiences. They presume a factually accurate rendering of the form and content of the cockfight (i.e., the propositions). What is missing is the local account and interpretation of the cockfight. This means we have only Geertz's theory of the cockfight. There is no way of knowing if his theory fits the interpretations held by the participants in this event.

Lindesmith, The Negative Case, and Analytic Interpretation

Further elaboration of analytic interpretation is required. I draw on the work of Alfred Lindesmith (1952, 1947), whose work on the logic of analytic induction closely parallels what I am terming analytic interpretation. Analytic induction (and interpretation) is the process of progressively defining and interpreting the phenomenon to be understood. Described abstractly, it involves the following steps:

1. Formulate a definition of the phenomenon.
2. Formulate an initial interpretation of the phenomenon.
3. Inspect a case, or a series of cases, in light of this interpretation.

4. Reformulate the interpretation as negative cases, or empirical irregularities emerge.
5. Continue this process until a universal, or all-encompassing, interpretation of every case has been formulated (see Denzin, 1978, p. 192; 1988, chap. 8).

Lindesmith (1952, p. 492) has termed this process analytic induction. I call it analytic interpretation because the inductive process (working from facts to regularities) is always interpretive (see Athens, 1984a, 1984b). Lindesmith explains (1952, p. 492):

> The principle that governs the selection of cases to test a theory is that the chances of discovering a decisive negative case should be maximized. The investigator who has a working hypothesis concerning his data becomes aware of certain areas of critical importance. . . . He knows that its weaknesses will be more clearly and quickly exposed if he proceeds to the investigation of these critical cases. This involves going out of one's way to look for negating evidence.

Here is an example from Lindesmith's (1947) research on opiate addiction. He was attempting to formulate a sociological theory of drug addiction. He began with the hypothesis that persons who knew they were taking a drug that was addictive could not become addicted. He also argued that persons would become addicted if they knew they were taking such drugs and if they had taken such drugs long enough to experience distress or withdrawal. This hypothesis was destroyed when he interviewed a physician who had taken morphine for several weeks, knew it, but did not become addicted. This negative case led Lindesmith to reformulate his hypothesis. He next argued that persons become addicts when they recognize and perceive the significance of withdrawal distress and then take the drug to remove the effects of withdrawal.

Lindesmith (1947, pp. 9-10) comments on his search for and use of negative cases:

> Each succeeding tentative formulation . . . was based on that which had preceded it. The eventual hypothesis altered the preceding formulations sufficiently to include the cases which earlier had appeared as exceptions to the theory postulated.

Lindesmith goes on to discuss how he explicitly sought out negative cases, both in his interviews with addicts and in the research literature. He argued that none of those cases contradicted the final hypothesis.

The intent of analytic interpretation is the formulation of interpretations that apply to every instance of the phenomenon examined. These interpretations must fit into a meaningful, interpretive whole, so that no case is excluded.

Problems and Advantages with Analytic Interpretation

Analytic interpretation suffers from four basic problems. First, it rests on a model of science that assumes hypotheses and the testing of theories. Second, it assumes that facts can be gathered and that these facts will offer tests of a theory. In this sense, the analytic approach often fails to deal with the socially constructed nature of a fact (Fielding and Fielding, 1986, p. 33). "Objective truth," or purely objective, noninterpretive tests of a theory can never be made (Patton, 1980, p. 331; Lincoln and Guba, 1985, p. 283). Third, it reduces the interpretive process to a set of decontextual, nonbiographical propositions. As a result, individual lived experiences disappear from the writer's text. Interpretive interactionism, as discussed in Chapter 1, rejects hypothesis and theory testing. Fourth, analytic interpretation, as noted above, suppresses the voices of the native. This leads to the production of monologic texts that displace the interpretations of natives.

There are, however, advantages to analytic interpretation, and these are balanced against the negative features just discussed. First, as an interpretive strategy, it forces the researcher clearly to specify the phenomenon and the research question under investigation (see Chapter 3). Second, it alerts the researcher to unique, or negative, cases, which might otherwise be ignored. Third, it forces the researcher constantly to judge his or her interpretations against lived experiences. Analytic interpretation is to be avoided if it leads to the writing of interpretations that are not dialogic, thick, and multivoiced.

Thick, Contextual, Interactional, Multivoiced
Interpretation: Ilongot Hunting Stories

Rosaldo's (1986, pp. 97-138) study of the hunting stories Ilongot men tell one another provides an illustration of a thick, multivoiced, contextual interpretation. The Ilongots number about 3500. They live in the upland northeast of Manila in the Philippines. They are headhunters, although they subsist by hunting deer and wild pig and by cultivating gardens. Their stories relate, with high drama, hunts, the killing of wild animals, risk-taking, fears of death, and the final victory of man over animal.

Rosaldo presents and analyzes several of these stories. Here is a portion of one of them:

> Let's go to a far place . . . and we'll hunt there. And after we've eaten game we'll go to the fork of the Mabu since it's there we can really hunt. . . . We're going to hunt the highest mountains [Rosaldo, 1986, p. 104].

Another story contains the following portions. A monster is addressing the headhunter's wives:

> Don't go and get their vaginas. . . . And their penises, Uh, they'll make us drunk. That's when, they say, friend, they chopped away, these Ilongots did, the ones raided, got lost, and came upon them. Now by stealth there they chopped them up [Rosaldo, 1986, p. 124].

Rosaldo offers the following interpretation of these stories:

> The stories these Ilongot men tell about themselves both reflect what actually happened and define the kinds of experiences they seek out on future hunts. Indeed, their very postures while hunting resemble those used in storytelling, and in this respect the story informs the experience of hunting. . . . Ilongot huntsmen experience themselves as the main characters in their own stories [Rosaldo, 1986, p. 134].

Rosaldo's reading of these stories fits them to the actual and imagined experiences of the hunters. He shows how their stories structure future hunts. In this sense, he joins a native theory of interpretation with his interpretation of the stories. Note that he does enquire into the "factual" accuracy of the stories. He treats them as accounts of events that may or may not have happened. In this sense, he reads the stories as symbolic expressions of the lived experiences of the Ilongot huntsmen.

Battered Wives as Victims

Johnson and Ferraro (1984, p. 119) are discussing the victimized self, which they define as "a complex mixture of feelings and thoughts based on the individual's overriding feeling of having been violated, exploited, or wronged by another person or persons." Based on their extensive analysis of the experiences of battered wives, they observe that the victimized self emerges during moments of existential threat, and it dissolves when one takes actions to construct new, safer living conditions. . . . [It] emerges when the rationalizations of violence and abuse begin to lose their power [Johnson and Ferraro, 1984, p. 121].

This interpretation is then contextualized, made biographical and inter-actional, through an interpretive reading of the stories battered wives tell about their marriages. Their final interpretive theory is multivoiced and dialogical. It builds on native interpretations and in fact simply articulates what is implicit in those interpretations. This is what thick interpretation is supposed to do. It brings to life and illuminates interpretive theories that already exist in the worlds of lived experience. I turn now to a discussion of understanding and its relationship to interpretation.

UNDERSTANDING

Interpretation is the clarification of meaning. Understanding is the process of interpreting, knowing, and comprehending the meaning that is felt, intended, and expressed by another (Denzin, 1984a, pp. 282-84). Interpretation precedes understanding. It has its meaning in the descrip-tion of another's actions within a framework that is meaningful to the person. Interpretation dissects units of experience into relevant segments (statements, sequences, actions) that have meaning for the other.

Just as description provides the framework for interpretation, so too does interpretation create the conditions for understanding. Under-standing is an interactional process. It requires that one person enter into the experience of another and "experience for herself the same or similar experiences experienced by another" (Denzin, 1984a, p. 137). "The subjective interpretation of another's emotional experience from one's own standpoint is central to emotional understanding" (Denzin, 1984a, p. 137). This means that shared and sharable emotionality lie at the center of the process of understanding. Two terms are basic to understanding: "interpretation" and "shared experience." A brief discussion of each is necessary.

Interpretation. Another's experiences cannot be understood until they have been interpreted. This means that the conditions of thick description must be present before meaningful interpretation can occur. The meaning of a violent act has no meaning out of context. In order to interpret that symbolic act, the reader must know what came before the violence. The reader must also know what followed that action. Once the context is established, the meaning of the act emerges. This is how description and interpretation work together.

Shared experience. Understanding, as suggested above, requires that one be able to enter into, or take the point of view of, another's experience. Mead (1934) called this "taking the attitude of the other." Various other terms have been used to describe this process: "sympathy," "empathy," "imagination," "Verstehen," "sympathetic understanding" (see Denzin, 1984a, p. 133). Whatever term is used, the meaning is essentially the same: projecting oneself into the experiences of another. This means that the other's experience must call out in the person experiences similar to those of the other. One must be able to see the other's experience from their point of view. This is what is meant by the phrase "living one's way into and through the life of the other." One must share, if only indirectly, in the emotional experiences of the other. If this is not done, shallow, empty, spurious, one-sided interpretation and understanding are produced.

Types of Understanding

There are two basic forms of understanding: cognitive and emotional (Denzin, 1984a, pp. 145-56). Emotional understanding moves along emotional lines as emotionality, self-feelings, and shared experience enter into the interactional-interpretative process. Cognitive understanding, in contrast, is rational, orderly, logical, and detached from emotional feeling. Cognitive understanding embraces emotion and displaces logic, reason, and rationality. In practice, it is difficult, if not impossible, to separate these two forms of understanding. This is the case because emotions and cognitions blur together in the person's stream of experience (James, 1890 [1950, vol. 1, pp. 185-87]).

These two forms of understanding may be dissected into two additional categories. The first is spurious understanding. This occurs when an individual has only superficially entered into the experiences of another. In spurious understanding, one projects their own understandings onto another. This often occurs because of an unwillingness to enter into the other's point of view. It may also occur because one mistakes one's own feelings for the feelings of the other. It may also be produced by thin, or inattentive, descriptions of the other's actions and experiences.

The second category of understanding that I wish to introduce is true or authentic emotional understanding. This occurs when one person has entered into the experiences of another, and reproduced, or felt, experiences similar to those felt by the other. This means that shared emotional experience underlies authentic emotional understanding.

Given the above distinctions, it is now possible to introduce one additional clarification. Corresponding to cognitive and emotional understandings are cognitive and emotional interpretations. Cognitive interpretations strip emotion from experience. They deal with the bare facts. They are based on thin descriptions. Emotional interpretations overflow with emotion and feeling.

An Illustration

Consider the following statement made by a recovering alcoholic who has slipped after six years of continuous sobriety. He is speaking to another A.A. member. He is in a detox center.

O.-P. "When I'm sober it doesn't bother me—that thing that happened 8 years ago (he molested a child). When I drink its right in front of me and I want to do it again. I go crazy thinking about it. Maybe that's why I started drinking again so I could think these insane, crazy thoughts. I don't know. Look where the drinking has got me now. A.'s (his ex-wife) got me over a barrel. She's got the house, the car, the money. Everything. What can I do? I can stay sober for a few weeks, then it all comes back to me. And then I drink. What can I do? Hell she made me so damned mad I hit her and threw her up against the wall. Now I can't go home.

I know I'm an alcoholic. I know the Program. I know how to stay sober but I can't. You know I stopped coming to meetings. I know I can't stop drinking after one drink. I even accept that I'm an alcoholic. I don't feel it in my gut though. I still think I can drink and control the stuff. I still want to drink. I can say the words 'I'm an alcoholic,' but I don't feel them. Hell, am I just crazy?" [Field conversation, as reported, August 1, 1985].

Each of the forms of understanding and interpretation, as discussed above, is present in this self-story. O. has a cognitive understanding and interpretation of his alcoholism. He emotionally understands the pain that he creates for himself when he drinks. But he does not feel deep inside himself that he is an alcoholic. He does not have an emotional understanding and interpretation of his situation. His understanding is superficial, or spurious. He dissociates himself from the negative experiences he creates when he drinks. He does not have a true or authentic grasp and understanding of what his alcoholism is doing and has done to him.

In a parallel manner, he cognitively grasps A.A.'s Program, but he has failed to live that Program into his life. He knows this. But he hasn't connected this cognitive knowledge to deep, emotional, self-understandings.

These forms of understanding and interpretation structure and organize the meanings and understandings persons form about themselves and others. They are present, in some form, in most if not all interactions a person moves through on a daily basis. Because they are woven into the fabric of everyday life, they must become part of the interpretive sociologist's vocabulary, but more than just this is involved. These forms and modes of understanding and interpretation define the essential goals of interpretation. *Stated succinctly, the goal of interpretation is to build true, authentic understandings of the phenomenon under investigation.* This is why thick description is so critical to interpretive studies. It creates verisimilitude, thereby allowing the reader to enter into the emotional experiences of those persons being studied.

Understanding and Applied Research

I have argued above (and see the Preface), that much applied, evaluative research assumes the formulation and existence of interpretations and understandings of the problems being addressed by a specific program. I have also argued for a consideration of the perspectives (local theories) of those persons served by a program. Evaluators form cognitive and emotional understandings that may be spurious, and they build interpretations that are often based on skewed, or biased, pictures of the phenomenon in question. Applied, evaluative research needs a theory of interpretation and understanding that is grounded in the distinctions made in this section.

Grief and a Headhunter's Rage

Let's return to Rosaldo and the Ilongot huntsmen, who are, as noted earlier, headhunters. When Rosaldo asked the men why they engaged in headhunting, he was invariably told that "the rage in bereavement could impel men to headhunt" (Rosaldo, 1984, p. 179). He always dismissed this answer as being too simplistic, thin, and implausible. In 1981, however, his wife Michelle Rosaldo fell to her death in the Philippines. They were doing research on the Ilongot at the time. He describes his experiences after this event:

I sobbed, but rage blocked the tears. . . . I felt in my chest the deep cutting pain of sorrow almost beyond endurance, the cadaverous cold of realizing the finality of death, the trembling beginning in my abdomen and spreading through my body as a form of wailing. . . . Writing in my journal six weeks after Shelly's death, I noted: If I ever return to anthropology by writing "Grief and a Headhunter's Rage. . . ." . . . Reflecting further on death, rage and headhunting, my journal goes on to describe my wish for the Ilongot solution; they are much more in touch with reality than Christians [Rosaldo, 1984, p. 184].

Out of his rage over his wife's death emerged the paper "Grief and a Headhunter's Rage"(Rosaldo, 1984). Rosaldo was not able to enter into and understand the Ilongot's experience until he had experienced an experience like theirs. Only then did he gain an emotional understanding of the headhunter's rage. When this occurred, he was able to grasp the meaning of the simple explanation the men gave for why they hunted heads after the death of a loved one.

The Lessons of Emotion

From Rosaldo's experience, several lessons can be learned. First, meaningful interpretation cannot be written until the observer has emotionally entered into and experienced the experiences he or she writes about. Second, readers cannot be expected to identify emotionally with and understand a set of written interpretations unless those interpretations are written in a way that elicits emotional identification and understanding. A reader cannot be expected to feel or understand something that a writer does not feel. Third, nonspurious emotional understandings can only be produced if the world of lived experience is brought alive on the pages of the writer's text. Fourth, emotional understandings cannot be created if a reader is not willing to enter into a writer's text and into the world of lived experience he or she depicts.

CONCLUSIONS

Forms and types of interpretation have been reviewed. The relationship between interpretation, description, and understanding has been discussed. The central place of emotionality in the interpretive process was stressed. In the next chapter, I turn to the main conclusions of this work.

7

Conclusion:
On Interpretive Interactionism

A review of the essential features of the interpretive approach to the study of problematic experience is given. Interpretive interactionism is located within the postmodern period of world history.

The basic question that has guided this investigation—how to do interpretive interactionism as a mode of qualitative research—has served a double purpose. On the one hand, the structures of interpretive research have been illuminated. On the other, this inquiry has revealed the centrality of the study of those life experiences that radically alter and change the meanings persons give to themselves and their experiences. In this conclusion, I review and offer reflections on these two purposes. If interpretive sociology is to advance its standing in the human disciplines, then the basic elements of interpretive interactionism demand further elaboration and presentation.

The following topics will be discussed: (1) the steps and phases of interpretation, (2) the structures of biographical experience, (3) reading and writing interpretation, (4) fiction and interpretation, and (5) interpretive interactionism in the postmodern period.

INTERPRETATION

The subject matter of interpretive studies is biographically meaningful experience. Borrowing from James Joyce, I have used the term "epiphany" to describe those interactional moments that leave positive and negative marks on people's lives. Often these moments are experienced as personal troubles that later become public issues (Mills, 1959). On other occasions epiphanies are experiences in positive terms, as when Martin Luther King heard the inner voice of Christ one night at his kitchen table. The interpretive interactionist seeks out subjects who have experienced epiphanies. I have offered several examples of such experiences in this text, including a murder, wife-battering, alcoholics seeking help for alcoholism, and husbands experiencing the death of their wives.

Steps to Interpretation

There are seven steps to the interpretive process (see Chapter 3), which I will briefly review.

Commonsense Causes and Finding the "How" Question

Interpretive research addresses "how," not "why," questions. This is the first phase in the interpretive process. It assumes that the answer to a how question will contain native, or subject, interpretations and explanations concerning "why" a certain experience happened. This requires a distinction between commonsense and scientific thinking on causal matters. Commonsense causal explanations "are based on matters which lie outside, but draw upon, scientific formulations" (Lindesmith, Strauss, and Denzin, 1988, p. 147). They are not predicated on scientific knowledge per se (Garfinkel, 1967, p. 271). Why, or causal, questions are resolved, then, into "everyday" causal explanations. As such, they typically take the form of accounts, excuses, and justifications for action (Lindesmith, Strauss, and Denzin, 1988, p. 146). Interpretive studies attempt to uncover the commonsense reasons for the meanings persons bring to the turning point moments in their lives. In so doing, they address the "hows" and the "whys" of existentially problematic experiences.

Personal Troubles and Public Issues

The location and framing of the "how" question always moves outward from the researcher's personal biography to those social settings where other persons experiencing the same personal trouble come together. The researcher goes to those settings and secures biographical accounts, personal experience narratives, and self-stories about the experience in question. As this process of listening and collecting stories unfolds, the investigator refines and shapes the research into a single statement. (I offered several examples of this process in Chapter 3.) The test of whether or not one understands one's problem is given in the ability to phrase it in a single statement as a question.

Deconstruction and Cultural Studies

As the "how" question takes shape, the researcher must work to free him- or herself from prior conceptions of the phenomenon being studied. If this is not done, the researcher is trapped by prior conceptions of the problem. This requires a serious, critical, deconstructive reading of the existing scientific and commonsense literature on the problem. This is the second step in interpretation. For example, in my studies of the American alcoholic, I was lead to read and evaluate critically the existing scientific theories of alcoholism. I also read and interpreted A.A.'s tests on alcoholism.

The world of lived experience is shaped by cultural understandings and cultural texts. These texts often give meaning to problematic experiences. For example, movies that focus on alcoholism and problematic drinkers show viewers how alcoholic drinkers drink. Some of these films show how A.A. works. Others show alcoholics in treatment centers. These films often speak to the lived experiences of alcoholics and their families (see Denzin, forthcoming-b).

Accordingly, a primary step in any interpretive study requires that the researcher collect the relevant cultural texts that describe the problematic experiences being studied. These texts will then be subjected to a deconstructive reading. Their recurring images of the phenomenon must be dissected. Their semiotic, signifying structures must be read (see Chapter 2). At the same time, they should be read through the lenses of feminist theory, so that the images of women that exist within them can be extracted. These texts will also presume a particular picture of work, money, and the economy. These conceptions must be identified (see Denzin, 1987c, for an example).

The deconstruction of a cultural text would, then, be semiotic, feminist, and culturally critical. It would identify the dominant meanings and codes in the text, and then perform a subversive, or critical, reading of the text, exposing in the process its underlying values and assumptions.

Capture, Bracketing, and Construction

The third, fourth, and fifth steps to interpretation are capture, bracketing, and construction. Capture involves going to the worlds of social experience where the "how" question occurs. It directs the investigator to obtain self-stories and personal experience narratives pertaining to the phenomenon in question. These narratives are symbolic expressions, shaped by the cultural and meaning systems of social groups. In capture, the researcher identifies how the cultural practices of social groups shape the narratives and symbolic expressions persons give to their experiences.

Bracketing leads the interpreter to inspect these symbolic expressions in terms of their essential, recurring features, such as the key elements in the stories battered women tell about their violent marriages. The isolation of these recurring features permits the researcher to determine how each person is a universal singular. That is, their stories are both like, and not like, any other story told by any other person who may have experienced the phenomenon in question.

Contextualizing

Having obtained native, narrative accounts of problematic experience, the investigator, in the phase of contextualizing, relocates the phenomenon back in the lives of the persons being studied. This is the sixth step to interpretation. It requires that attention be given to individual biography and to the effects of turning point experiences on these individuals and their social relationships. Contextualizing anchors the accounts of problematic experience in the relational world of the subject.

Writing Interpretation

Given that the researcher has moved through the above six steps, he or she must next address the problem of writing interpretation. This is the seventh phase of interpretation. (Of course, it occurs in each of the above phases, in the form of field notes, memos, working papers, and the like. See Strauss, 1987, chap. 9.) I will take up the problem of writing interpretation in greater detail below (and see the discussion in Chapter 6).

BIOGRAPHICAL EXPERIENCE

Meaningful biographical experience occurs in turning point interactional episodes. In these existentially problematic moments, human character is revealed, and human lives are shaped, sometimes irrevocably. It is necessary to discuss the structures of these moments and the experiences that flow from them.

Four Experiential Structures

It is possible to identify four major structures, or types of existentially problematic moments, or epiphanies, in the lives of individuals. First, there are those moments that are major and touch every fabric of a person's life. Their effects are immediate and long term. Second, there are those epiphanies that represent eruptions, or reactions, to events that have been going on for a long period of time. Third are those events that are minor yet symbolically representative of major problematic moments in a relationship. Fourth, and finally, are those episodes whose effects are immediate, but their meanings are only given later, in retrospection, and in the reliving of the event. I give the following names to these four structures of problematic experience: (1) the major epiphany, (2) the cumulative epiphany, (3) the illuminative, minor epiphany, and (4) the relived epiphany. (Of course, any epiphany can be relived and given new retrospective meaning.) These four types may, of course, build upon one another. A given event may, at different phases in a person's or relationship's life, be first, major, then minor, and then later relived. A cumulative epiphany will, of course, erupt into a major event in a person's life. I offer examples of each type.

The Major Epiphany

Recall once again Raskolnikov's murder of the pawnbroker. In Chapter 1, I used Dostoyevsky's account of this event as an example of how thick description is written. Readers of *Crime and Punishment* will know that this murder was a major turning point experience in Raskolnikov's life. It led to his arrest, trial, imprisonment, and subsequent religious experience in the prison camp.

The Cumulative Epiphany

Now reconsider Johnson and Ferraro's battered woman (Chapter 6) who had lived with her violent husband for years, until one day he put a gun to her head. On that day, she sued for separation of property and left her husband. This woman's turning point experience did not just happen, it was the result of an accumulation of past experiences that culminated in a single moment.

The Illuminative, Minor Epiphany

Next, the following interactional episode: Four persons are seated around a family kitchen table. A window looks out into the backyard onto a bird feeder. The individuals are Jack, a 55-year-old bachelor, his girlfriend, Sharon, Jack's mother Mae, and Paul, a 47-year-old recently divorced friend of Jack. Jack has brought his new girlfriend home to meet his mother. Paul has recently met Mae. Mae and Jack have been fighting for years over Jack's inability to settle down and become a respectable, married man. The following conversation was reported.

Mae: Looking out the window. "My word, that bird feeder's empty. Seems like its always empty these days."

Jack: "I'll fill it Ma. No problem. Birdseed still where it always was?"

Mae: "Ya, now don't go and fill it more than half-way up." Turning to Sharon and Paul, in front of Jack "He never listens to me. He always spills seed on the ground. He's just like a little boy."

Jack: Goes out the backdoor, gets the birdseed from the wood shed, takes the sack of seed to the bird feeder, pulls the sack into the feeder, until it overflows, with seed streaming down to the ground.

Mae: Shouting, through the walls of the living room, "You idiot, I said half-full! Can't you remember anything! He never listens to me. Its always been like this. Why can't he do what I want him to?"

This interaction between a mother and her son may be read as revealing underlying tensions and conflicts in their relationship. It is not a turning point moment, yet it brings to the surface and illuminates what has been, in the past, a break, or rupture, in the relationship. The son has refused to live his life as his mother wants him to. His refusal to follow her instructions on how to put birdseed in the bird feeder symbolically speaks to this rupture. It is a minor epiphany.

The Relived, Retrospectively Meaningful Epiphany

Finally, the death of Michelle Rosaldo in 1981: The meaning of this death to her husband, Renato, was still being determined two years after it happened. The death was a major event in his life. It has led him to reinterpret his entire relationship to the field of anthropology.

Studying Epiphanies

In Chapter 2, I discussed in detail how the researcher obtains and interprets biographically problematic experience. This involved a detailed discussion of the biographical method, including securing stories of problematic experiences. Little needs to be added to that discussion. As the investigator grounds his or her study in lived experience, major, cumulative, minor, and relived epiphanies will be observed and told about. What requires elaboration, however, is the point that each of the above types of the epiphany must, as much as possible, be collected and studied within any interpretive investigation. This is the case if a thickly described and thickly interpreted picture of problematic experienced is to be produced. This is what is involved in doing existential ethnography (see Denzin, forthcoming-a, chap. 7).

READING AND WRITING INTERPRETATION

A brief analysis of reading and writing interpretation is necessary. This means that I must discuss readers, writers, and texts. A "text," in the context, refers to any printed, visual, oral, or auditory (i.e., musical) statement that is available for reading, viewing, or hearing. Texts are always authored. A text may be authored by ordinary, interacting individuals, or it may be professionally produced by scholars or professionals. A "reader" is a person who reads, hears, sees, and interprets a text. A reader may be an ordinary person, or a professional, or a scholar. A "writer," or author, is a person, agency, or institution that creates a text that is read, seen, or heard by others. An author may be an ordinary person telling a person about her life, or a professional writer, such as an ethnographer, a sociologist, or a critic. Readers, writers, and texts exist within larger cultural, political, and ideological contexts (Barthes, 1967). A political, ideological process structures the creation of readers, writers, and texts. Readers first.

Readers

In Chapter 6, I argued that the writers of interpretive texts require willing readers. By this I meant that a reader must be willing to enter into the emotional fields of experience that are contained in a writer's text. Coleridge (1817 [1973, p. 516]) termed this the willing suspension of disbelief, that is, a readiness on the reader's part to trust or have faith in the writer. But more is involved.

A reader brings meaning to and creates the text that is read. This means that there is no absolute point or degree zero (Barthes (1953 [1973]) in a text. Three issues are involved in this assertion. First, texts are not unambiguous in their meaning. Readers bring to them their own experiences with the experiences that are written about. Second, they bring their own understandings and interpretations of the words that are used in the text. Third, as they emotionally and cognitively interact with a text, they may be drawn to it, repulsed by it, bored by it, disagree with it, not understand it, or completely accept it. They do not have a neutral relationship to the text that they read.

Here is the author of an oral text challenging his listeners. He is speaking to an A.A. meeting.

> You may not like what I'm about to say. You may hate me, But that's all right. I've lied. I've cheated, I've stolen things. I've been violent to people, once I broke a man's back because he wouldn't give me a hit. I don't care what you think, I'm here for me [Denzin, 1987b, p. 191].

In this statement, the speaker, as the writer, or author, of his own text, anticipates his audience's repulsion to what he is about to say. He knows that there are no neutral listeners.

The following statement by a member of the group who heard this man speak confirms his prediction.

> What was he trying to do? Who does he think he is? Does he think he's unique? How long has he been in treatment anyway? When's he goin to learn to talk for himself and not for who he think's listen'n to him? I didn't believe him anyway. I have a lotta trouble with people like him.

Here the audience member, as a reader of an oral text, makes a judgment about the text and the speaker.

Readers constitute the text as they read it and interact with it. This means that, for any given reader, some texts are more readerly than others. I prefer texts with thick descriptions that evoke emotional interpretations. Other readers like clear, unambiguous, unemotional texts.

Writers and Texts

The texts that writers produce are shaped by four forces, or processes: (1) language, (2) ideology, (3) myth, and (4) history, convention, and style.

Language

Language, of course, structures the process of writing. Words define the objects and the experiences that are written about. But language, with its syntactical and semantical structures (i.e., rules of sentence construction, rules of meaning), dictate what a writer can write. I can't call a cow a dog, for example, and convey to you that I am writing about a cow and not a dog. I can say, "Cow writing about am a I," and convince you that this is a sentence that states "I am writing about a cow." The rules of language structure what I write and what you read and interpret.

Every word that I write, every object that I refer to, is already filled with meaning. If I write about *experience*, or *epiphanies*, you bring your meanings (as I noted above) to these words. If you consult a dictionary, you will find many different meanings of these two words. Words overflow with meaning. What a writer writes, then is predetermined, in part, by what his or her language allows to be written. The same holds, of course, for readers.

Ideology and Myth

Barthes (1957 [1972]) reminds us that the culture- and knowledge-making institutions of a society—including the law, medicine, religion, the physical and social sciences, the humanities, the arts, the mass media, and the arts—produce and reproduce knowledge and records of social events that structure and give meaning to everyday life. These representations, records, and texts often lend a sense of "naturalness" to the events that have been recorded and written about. In the process, they "dress up a reality which, even though it is the one we live in, is undoubtedly determined by history" (Barthes, 1957 [1972, p. 11]). By displaying events and happenings as natural occurrences, nature and history are confused, for "what-goes-without-saying" (Barthes, 1957 [1972, p. 1]) in a display or text is ideologically shaped. This means that these works can not be read as "literal" representations of the social situations to which they refer. They are ideological representations of the social situations to which they refer. They are ideological representations of the social and reflect the biases and prejudices of their producers.

Gender

These representations often reflect a patriarchal, male, interpretive bias. They view the social world through the male gaze and male voice. They often equate masculinity with objectivity and femininity with subjectivity. In the process, they "obscure the patriarchal bias at the core of science" (Cook and Fonow, 1986. p. 6). Like myth, these documents have reproduced the gender stratification systems of postmodern society.

Myth

The representations that social scientists write may be likened to "myths." A myth is a text that is based on everyday phenomenon. A myth tells a story that offers, or contains, an explanation of some fact, phenomenon, or event. It presents those phenomena in a readable language that makes them seem sensible, natural, orderly, and understandable. A myth presents "truths" about reality.

Numerous examples of myth have been given in earlier chapters. In Chapter 5, I quoted from Collins's interpretation of the "rating and dating complex" in American society. In that statement, Collins offered an explanation for the presence of force in the dating system. He implicitly suggested that some women allow themselves to be raped if they think marriage to a desirable mate will be the outcome. This is a mythical statement. It presents accounts of things and happenings.

Myth often distorts and reproduces biases and prejudices that exist within the larger culture. Collins's account of force in the dating relationship can be read as saying that women sexually encourage men to take advantage of them. Taken to its extreme, this interpretation holds women responsible for being raped. It must be noted that all myth is ideological. It either supports the status quo or challenges the current arrangement of things in the social world. Myth on the right supports the status quo. Myth on the left often calls for radical social change (Barthes, 1957 [1972, pp. 145-50]).

History, Convention, and Style

More than words, language, ideology, and myth shape what goes into a text. Convention and style also influence what is written. Convention refers to established ways or modes of presentation. Style refers to variations within a convention, and is often associated with the work of a particular person or group. Historically, in the social sciences, two dominant writing conventions have prevailed: the scientific article and the humanistic essay. The scientific article builds on the social science myth of objectivity. It is often filled with words like "hypothesis," "hypothesis testing," "reliability," "validity," "generalization," "standard error," and so forth. First-person statements are typically absent. The text is written as if it objectively maps the empirical reality under inspection. Within the conventional structure of the scientific article, individual authors establish their own styles of presentation.

The humanistic essay form is often written in the first person. It extends the myth of subjectivity and the importance of studying human subjects. It lacks the rigorous organization of the scientific article, and avoids terms like "hypothesis testing" and "reliability." This convention, as used in the social sciences, draws the writer (and the reader) more closely into literary styles of writing. Howard S. Becker (1986a, p. 105) comments on his writing style:

> Sometime in the seventies, I began to develop literary pretensions and ambitions. I think this started when a friend who was a "real writer" [a writer, that is, of fiction] said some things about some drafts of an essay I was writing on art worlds. . . . I began experimenting with a kind of organization I had barely been aware of before.

Styles of Writing Interpretation

Interpretive writing is located, of course, within the humanistic writing tradition in the social sciences. In the previous chapter, I identified several styles, or ways, of writing interpretation. These included monologic, dialogic, polyphonic, analytic, factual-descriptive, and interpretive-narrative styles. Now I want to make matters slightly more complicated by introducing three additional writing styles. I will call these (1) mainstream realism, (2) interpretive realism, and (3) descriptive realism (see Rabinow, 1986, pp. 234-61).

Mainstream realism. Mainstream realism assumes that the author of a text can give an objective accounting, or portrayal, of the realities of a group or an individual. It attempts to capture the objective elements of a culture and social structure. A realist study might use, for example, traditional concepts like kinship, economic and religious systems, norms and values, deviance and social control. It would then map these structures into the experiences that the researcher has observed. Mainstream realism assumes that structures such as those given in concepts like kinship, or political system, in fact exist in the group being studied. It also assumes that an "objective" reading of these structures can be given. Mainstream realism leads to the production of monologic, analytic, interpretive texts (see the Collins discussion above).

Interpretive realism. Interpretive realism describes that mode of writing where the author presumes to be able to interpret the realities of other people. Clifford Geertz is known for producing texts like this

(Crapanzano, 1986). The observer's interpretations displace those of the native. Interpretive realist texts often have the flavor of "I was there and this is what I experienced." This experiential tone is filtered through the experiences of the observer, however, not the native.

Descriptive Realism

In descriptive realism, the writer attempts to allow the world being interpreted to interpret itself. Here the writer employs the strategy of using multiple voices to speak from his or her text. The film critic Michiko Kakutani (1987, p. 1, 50) discusses John Huston's film *The Dead*, which is based on James Joyce's short story "The Dead." He argues that Joyce's early stories introduced Huston to the possibilities of realism. He then quotes Wieland Schulz-Keil, one of the producers of *The Dead*, who in a conversation stated that perhaps Huston

> learned from Joyce that a story should not attempt to interpret life, but should describe an order and an interpretation arising from life itself. Joyce and Huston show views of life as they emerge from their stories' characters. These interpretations can be discerned in the thought of the characters, their consciousness and . . . in their words and actions. It is not one view but many that overlap, complement and contradict each other. This is realism in action. It explains . . . the absence of a homogeneous, identifiable style in the work of the two authors. The style changes with the characters whose view of life . . . is revealed in any instance.

Descriptive realism is dialogic and polyphonic. It tells the native's stories in his or her own words. It allows interpretation to emerge from the stories that are told. It reveals the conflictual, contradictory nature of lived experience and suggests that no single story or interpretation will fully capture the problematic events that have been studied. Descriptive realism assumes that reasonable, plausible, workable theories and accounts of experience can be given by those persons who experience the event or events in question. After all, it is their lives that are being told about.

Here is an example from Vincent Crapanzano's 1980 book, *Tuhami: Portrait of a Moroccan*. Tuhami is a Moroccan tile maker. He told Crapanzano stories about his life that were fantasies, made-up accounts of experiences that could not have "really" happened. Yet Tuhami believed them and acted as if they were real. Consider the following:

That is what I told you yesterday. . . .
When I dream, I dream of things that are true, I dream and fight. I never
call to anyone but Allah . . . today I find that my limbs are strong . . . when
you burn spices, it strangles the others in the neck. . . . I'll have my freedom
because I saw Mme Jolan in my room. The moment I woke up, I saw her
[Crapanzano, 1980, p. 172].

Tuhami believes that what he dreams is real. He lives his life in terms of
experiences like this. He is able to distinguish between the "reality" of
personal history and the "truth of autobiography" (Crapanzano, 1980,
p. 5). The reality of personal history refers to some correspondence
between a text or narrative and some set of external, observable
experiences. The truth of an autobiography "resides within the text itself
without any regard to any external criteria save, perhaps the I of the
narrator" (Crapanzano, 1980, p. 5). Descriptive realism attempts to
capture autobiographical narratives (personal experience and self-
stories). These stories may or may not be true in any objectively
verifiable sense. They have meaning for and structure the life experiences
of their narrators. This brings me, finally, to the topic of fiction and
interpretation.

FICTION AND INTERPRETATION

Fiction, usually a story, or a narrative, is something made up out of
experience. A fiction is not opposed to something that it is true
(Clifford, 1986, p. 6). It is fashioned out of something that was thought,
imagined, acted out, or experienced. All interpretation is fictional in the
sense that it involves either the observer's or the subject's accounting of
what has occurred or of what something means. Fictions are true, but
true only within the stories that contain them. If something can be
imagined, it is real (Sartre, 1948, pp. 165-66; Denzin, 1984a, p. 211).
Tuhami's fictions, his dreams, and his fantasies are true; true, that is, for
him. These are the only truths that are sought in descriptive, realist,
existential ethnographies.

There are five implications to the above assertions that all interpretation is fictional. First, writers of interpretation must free themselves
from the erroneous preconception that they do not write mythical
fictions. Second, they must learn how to experiment with modes of
writing that are not tied to mainstream and interpretive realist criteria of

evaluation. Third, they must learn to listen to the "truthful, fictional" stories that natives tell. Fourth, they must learn how to hear these stories for what they are—that is, as meaningful accounts of existentially problematic experience. Fifth, alternative ways of presenting interpretation must be experimented with, including film, novels, drama and plays, songs, music, poetry, dance, paintings, photography, sculpture, pottery, toolmaking, and architecture. Each of these representational forms speak to the problem of presenting and doing interpretation. By experimenting with them, the interpreter enlarges his or her interpretive horizon. In so doing, he or she opens wider the windows of interpretation that look out into the worlds that have been studied. This means that interpretive interactionists must direct their studies of life into the postmodern period.

INTERPRETIVE INTERACTIONISM IN THE POSTMODERN PERIOD

"All classic social scientists have been concerned with the salient characteristics of their time" (Mills, 1959, p. 165). This means that they have been preoccupied with how history, and human nature, is being made within their historical moment. They have been concerned with the variety and types of individuals—men, women, and children—who have died or prevailed and lives in their historical present (Mills, 1959, p. 165). Marx, Weber, William James, Simmel, G. H. Mead, Margaret Mead, Gregory Bateson, Veblen, Cooley, Durkheim, and Mills each confronted these problems.

At least four epochs have captured human history: Antiquity, the Middle Ages, the Modern Age, and now the Fourth Epoch, or the postmodern period (Mills, 1959, p. 166). The last two decades of the twentieth century find us in the middle of the postmodern period, which began after World War II. This is the age of multinational corporations, of satellite communication systems, of an interdependent world economy, of single-parent families, day-care children, working mothers, the "graying" of America, the threat of nuclear annihilation, environmental destruction, the increased domination of biomedical technologies, problems with drug and alcohol addiction, and armed confrontations in the Middle East, Central America, and South Africa.

The postmodern age is one in which advertising, the mass media, especially television, and the computer have gained ever greater control over human lives and human experience. This is an age in which problematic experiences are given meaning in the media. Social objects have become commodities. Human experience and social relationships have also become commodities, as anyone who scans the travel sections of the Sunday newspapers, with their supplements on holiday tours, can quickly confirm. It is an age marked by nostalgia for the past. Extreme self-interest and personal gain, coupled with the ostentatious display of material possessions, characterize the life-style of many today. At the same time, massive anxieties at the level of the personal and the social are felt. According to some sources, one in three American adults are now seeking psychotherapy and other forms of professional help for their individual problems. This is an age of personal unrest in which individual, family, sexual, leisure, and work experiences are becoming more and more problematic (Bellah et al., 1985).

Interpretive interactionism in the postmodern period is committed to understanding how this historical moment universalizes itself in the lives of interacting individuals. Each person, and each relationship, studied is assumed to be a *universal singular*, or a single instance of the universal themes that structure the postmodern period. Each person is touched by the mass media, by alienation, by the economy, by the new family and child-care systems, by the increasing technologizing of the social world, and by the threat of nuclear annihilation. Interpretive interactionism fits itself to the relation between the individual and society, to the nexus of biography and society. Interpretive interactionism attempts to show how individual troubles and problems become public issues. In the discovery of this nexus, it attempts to bring alive the existentially problematic, often hidden, and private experiences that give meaning to everyday life as it is lived in this moment in history.

To make the invisible more visible to others is, after all, a major goal of the interpreter (Merleau-Ponty, 1968). This means that we want to capture the stories of everyday persons as they tell about the pains, the agonies, the emotional experiences, the small and the large victories, the traumas, the fears, the anxieties, the dreams, fantasies, and the hopes in their lives. We want to make those stories available to others. To repeat what I said at the end of Chapter 1, citing C. W. Mills and William Faulkner, the sociologist's voice must speak to the terrible and magnificent world of human experience in the last years of the twentieth century. This is what this book has been all about.

GLOSSARY OF TERMS

Account: an explanation of a set of actions or experiences.

Analytic interpretation: imposes an abstract, often causal scheme on a set of experiences or events, usually derived from a scientific theory.

Biographical experience: experience that shapes a person's life, experience being how reality presents itself to consciousness (Bruner, 1986, p. 6); the subject matter of interpretive interactionism; see "problematic experience."

Biography: a written account or history of the life of an individual; the art of writing such accounts.

Bracketing: isolating the key, essential features of the processes under inspection.

Capture: securing instances of the phenomenon being studied.

Cause: an accounting of a set of actions or experiences, may be common sense or scientific.

Contextualizing: relocating bracketed phenomenon back in the worlds of lived experience.

Construction: follows bracketing, involves putting the key elements of a phenomenon back together again, in temporal order; leads to contextualizing.

Convention: an established mode of presentation, may be humanistic or scientific; there are styles within conventions.

Cultural studies: that field of inquiry that takes as its subject matter the culture-making institutions of a society and their productions of meaning; interpretive studies examine the problematic lived experiences shaped by these culture-making institutions.

Deconstruction: critical analysis and interpretation of prior studies and representations of the phenomenon in question.

Description: art of describing, giving an account of anything in words; types—thick and thin.

Descriptive realism: allowing the world studied to interpret itself; leads to dialogic and polyphonic texts.

Dialogic interpretation: an interpretation that is a dialogue between the observer and those studied, usually multivoiced, or *polyphonic*; contrasted to *monologic interpretation*, which suppresses the voices of those studied.

Engulfing: building an interpretation that includes all that is known to be relevant about a phenomenon; always incomplete.

Epiphany: moment of problematic experience that illuminates personal character, and often signifies a turning point in a person's life; types—major, minor, illuminative, relived.

Ethnography: the study of lived experiences, involving description and interpretation.

Expression: how individual and interactional experience is framed and articulated; expressions of experience are symbolic and include drama, performances, ritual, and storytelling (see Bruner, 1986, pp. 6-7).

Existential ethnography: that mode of ethnography that collects and studies problematic, turning point experiences in the lives of ordinary people.

Feminist critique: locates gender asymmetry at the center of the social world, including the world of social inquiry; there is no gender-free knowledge; the same argument holds for race and ethnicity as processes that also shape inquiry and experience in basic ways.

Fiction: a story or narrative made up out of experience; fictions are always true within the stories that contain them; all interpretation is mythical and fictional.

Gloss: a superficial, partial rendering or accounting of a phenomenon; types—everyday and scientific.

Hermeneutic circle: all interpreters are caught in the circle of interpretation; it is impossible to be free of interpretations, or to conduct "purely" objective studies.

Ideology: an accounting of the way things are and should be, typically political; involves the manipulation of ideas about the world in which we live.

Ideographic research: research that treats each individual as a *universal singular*, seeks to study experience from within; also called *emic*, to be contrasted to *etic, nomothetic* studies that attempt to generalize across subjects.

Informed reader: a reader who knows the language spoken in a story, who knows the biography of the storyteller, who is able to take the teller's point of view, who has had the experiences told about in the story, who is willing to take the responsibility for his or her interpretations of the story, and who is knowledgeable in the full range of interpretative theories that could be brought to bear upon the story in question.

Interaction: symbolically taking the perspective of another, and acting on that perspective; interaction is always emergent.

Interactional slice: an interactional sequence that has been recorded.

Interactional text: occurs whenever an individual is located in a social situation.

Interpret: to explain the meaning of, to translate into intelligible or familiar terms; leads to understanding.

Interpretation: the act of interpreting; creates the conditions for understanding, may be emotional, cognitive, spurious, or authentic; is a temporal process; is always symbolic; types—thin, thick, native, observer, analytic, monologic, dialogic, polyphonic, descriptive-contextual, relation-interactional; all interpretations should be relational, interactional, contextual, dialogic, and polyphonic.

Interpreter: one who interprets, or translates meaning, for others; types—native and scientific, or well-informed experts.

Interpretive: to explain the meaning of; the act of interpreting, or conferring meaning.

Interpretive biographical method: that method which utilizes personal experience narrative, self-stories, and personal histories.

Interpretive evaluation: interpretive, naturalistic, program evaluation, policy-making research that makes the investigator an advocate, or partisan, for those served by applied programs.

Interpretive interactionism: the point of view that illuminates and confers meaning on problematic symbolic interaction; seeks to use a concept-free mode of discourse, based on first-order concepts from lived experience.

Interpretive process: involves six steps, or phases—framing the research question, deconstruction, capture, bracketing, construction, and contextualization.

Interpretive realism: that mode of writing where the author presumes to be able to interpret the realities of other people; closely related to mainstream realism, usually associated with monologic texts.

Interpretive studies: that interpretive project which takes as its subject matter biographically meaning experience.

Interpretive theory: a theory, interpretation, or accounting of a set of experiences; may be native, or scientific.

Issue: a personal trouble that becomes a public problem.

Life: the biographical experiences of a named person; a life has two levels, the surface and the deep.

Lived experience: the world of actual experience.

Lay theory: an interpretive account of experience developed by the person having the experience.

Mainstream realism: a writing style that attempts to report "objectively" on the realities of a group.

Meaning: what an experience means to a person, defined in terms of intentions and consequences; meaning is always triadic, involving interaction between a person, an object, and action taken toward the object; meaning is interactional, interpretive, open-ended, often ambiguous, inconclusive, and conflictual.

Myth: a text, usually a story, that presents "truths" about reality, usually ideologically shaped, may be on the left or the right; may be produced by ordinary people, or by professional observers of society.

Narrator: a person who tells a story.

Narrative: a story that has a plot, a beginning, a middle, and an end.

Naturalism: locating inquiry in the natural worlds of everyday social experience and using methods that respect this world.

Participant observation: observing and participating in the worlds of lived experience that one is studying; involves learning how to listen, see, and talk within the worlds being studied.

Personal experience narrative: a story that relates the self of the teller to a significant set of personal experiences that have already occurred.

Personal history: reconstructions of a life based on interviews, conversations, self- and personal experience stories.

Postmodern: two meanings—life since World War II, and that mode of discourse that seeks to write life experiences in the postmodern period.

Problematic experience: epiphanies or moments of crisis in a person's life.

Problematic interaction: interactional experience that gives primary meaning to a subject's life.

Progressive-regressive method: also called the critical-interpretive method; seeks to locate and understand a class of subjects within a given historical moment; moves forward to the conclusion of a set of experiences, and then backward to the historical, cultural, and biographical conditions that moved the subject to take, or experience, the actions being studied.

Pure interpretation: interpretation for the purposes of building meaningful interpretations and understandings of social, cultural, and biographical problematics.

Reader: one who reads, hears, sees, and interprets a text.

Reality: the world of lived experience.

Realism: the relationship between a text and the world of lived experience; produces three writing styles—mainstream realism, interpretive realism, and descriptive realism.

Research question: always phrased as a "how," not a "why," question.

Self-story: a narrative that creates and interprets a structure of experience that is being told about; the self of the teller is at the center of the story.

Semiotic analysis: a method for reading the meaning of words and signs within narrative and interactional texts; it directs attention to the codes, metaphors, and metonymies that organize the text; it suggests that texts are structured in terms of oppositions (e.g., male versus female). Any text contains multiple, often contradictory meanings and messages that a semiotic analysis helps to disclose.

Social type: an individual who represents through his or her actions a typical way of acting in a social situation.

Style: variations within a writing or speaking convention.

Symbolic interaction: human interactional experience mediated by language and symbols.

Temporal mapping: connecting individuals to social situations; includes determining temporal sequencing and the location of the situations where persons come together; focuses on *who* does *what* with *whom, when* and *where.*

Text: any printed, visual, oral, or auditory statement that is available for reading, viewing, or hearing; readers create texts as they read them; the meaning of a text is always indefinite; readers, writers, and texts are shaped by the forces of language, ideology, myth, history, convention, and style.

Theory: an interpretive structure that renders a set of experiences meaningful and understandable; may be lay or professional, always derives from the cultural understandings of a group.

Thick description: capturing the meanings and experiences that have occurred in a problematic situation; reports meanings, intentions, history, biography, and relevant relational, interactional and situational processes in a rich, dense, detailed manner; creates the conditions for interpretation and understanding; contrasted to *thin description*, which is factual; types— micro, macro-historical, biographical, situational, relational, interactional, intrusive, incomplete, glossed, purely descriptive, descriptive, and interpretive.

Thick interpretation: builds on thick description; attempts to take the reader to the heart of the experience being studied.

Thin description: a description lacking detail; a simple reporting of acts, independent of intentions or the circumstances that organize an action; a gloss; types—everyday glosses, social science glosses, typified.

Trouble: a problem that occurs within the immediate world of experience of the person; personal troubles are often translated into public issues and into institutional responses that are intended to deal with them; examples include wife-battering, rape, problem drinking, alcoholism, drug addiction, and AIDs.

Understand: to comprehend, or grasp, the meaning of an interpreted phenomenon, may be emotional, or cognitive, or both; an interactional, emotional process, involving shared experience that may produce spurious or authentic understanding; the goal of interpretation is to build authentic, shareable understandings of the phenomenon under investigation; also called *verisimilitude*.

Universal singular: every person is a singular instance of the universal themes that structure his or her moment in history.

Writer: a person, agency, or institution that creates a text that is read, seen, or heard by others; a writer is also called an author; a writer-author may be an ordinary person, or a professional (e.g., an ethnographer, sociologist, anthropologist, novelist, painter).

REFERENCES

Adler, Patricia A. and Peter Adler. 1987. *Membership Roles in Field Research.* Newbury Park, CA: Sage.

Agar, Michael H. 1986. *Speaking of Ethnography.* Beverly Hills, CA: Sage.

Alcoholics Anonymous. 1953. *Twelve Steps and Twelve Traditions.* New York: Alcoholics Anonymous World Services, Inc.

———. 1957. *Alcoholics Anonymous Comes of Age: A Brief History of A.A.* New York: Alcoholics Anonymous World Services, Inc.

———. 1967. *As Bill Sees It: The A.A. Way of Life—Selected Writings of A.A.'s Co-Founder.* New York: Alcoholics Anonymous World Services, Inc.

———. 1976. *Alcoholics Anonymous.* New York: Alcoholics Anonymous World Services, Inc.

———. 1986. *Eastern United States A.A. Directory.* New York: Alcoholics Anonymous World Services, Inc.

Allport, Gordon W. 1942. *The Use of Personal Documents in Psychological Research.* New York: Social Science Research Council.

Athens, Lonnie H. 1984a. "Blumer's Method of Naturalistic Inquiry: A Critical Examination." Pp. 241-57 in *Studies in Symbolic Interaction.* Vol. 5, edited by N. K. Denzin. Greenwich, CT: JAI Press.

———. 1984b. "Scientific Criteria for Evaluating Qualitative Studies." Pp. 259-68 in *Studies in Symbolic Interaction.* Vol. 5, edited by N. K. Denzin. Greenwich, CT: JAI Press.

Bakhtin, M. M. 1981. *The Dialogic Imagination,* edited by Michael Holquist. Austin: University of Texas Press.

Barthes, Roland. 1967. *Elements of Semiology.* New York: Hill and Wang.

———. 1972. *Mythologies.* New York: Hill and Wang. [Originally published 1957]

———. 1973. *Writing Degree Zero.* New York: Hill and Wang. [Originally published 1953]

Bateson, Gregory. 1972. *Steps to an Ecology of Mind.* San Francisco: Chandler.

———. 1979. *Mind and Nature.* New York: Dutton.

Baudrillard, Jean. 1983. *Simulations.* New York: Semiotext(e), Inc.

Becker, Howard S. 1960. "Notes on the Concept of Commitment." *American Journal of Sociology* 66:32-40.

———. 1964. "Personal Change in Adult Life." *Sociometry* 27:40-53.

———. 1967. "Introduction." Pp. 1-31 in *Social Problems: A Modern Approach,* edited by Howard S. Becker. New York: John Wiley.

———. 1970. *Sociological Work.* Chicago: Aldine.

———. 1973. *Outsiders.* New York: Free Press.

———. 1982. *Art Worlds.* Berkeley: University of California Press.

———. 1986a. *Writing for Social Scientists: How to Start and Finish Your Thesis, Book or Article.* Chicago: University of Chicago Press.

———. 1986b. *Doing Things Together: Selected Papers.* Evanston, IL: Northwestern University Press.

———, Blanche Geer, Everett C. Hughes, and Anselm Strauss. 1961. *Boys in White: Student Culture in Medical School.* Chicago: University of Chicago Press.

Becker, Howard S. and Irving Louis Horowitz. 1986. "Radical Politics and Sociological Observation: Observations on Methodology and Ideology." Pp. 83-102 in *Doing Things Together: Selected Papers*, edited by Howard S. Becker. Evanston, IL: Northwestern University Press.

Bellah, Robert N. et al. 1985. *Habits of the Heart: Individualism and Commitment in American Life*. Berkeley: University of California Press.

Berger, Arthur Asa. 1982. *Media Analysis Techniques*. Beverly Hills, CA: Sage.

Bertaux, Daniel. 1981a. "Introduction." Pp. 5-15 in *Biography and Society: The Life History Approach in the Social Sciences*, edited by D. Bertaux. Beverly Hills, CA: Sage.

———. 1981b. "From the Life-History Approach to the Transformation of Sociological Practice." Pp. 29-46 in *Biography and Society: The Life History Approach in the Social Sciences*, edited by D. Bertaux. Beverly Hills, CA: Sage.

——— and Isabelle Bertaux-Wiame. 1981. "Life Stories in the Bakers' Trade." Pp. 169-90 in *Biography and Society: The Life History Approach in the Social Sciences*, edited by Daniel Bertaux. Beverly Hills, CA: Sage.

Bertaux-Wiame, Isabelle. 1981. "The Life History Approach to the Study of Internal Migration." Pp. 249-66 in *Biography and Society: The Life History Approach in the Social Sciences*, edited by Daniel Bertaux. Beverly Hills, CA: Sage.

Blumer, Herbert. 1937. "Social Psychology." Pp. 36-72 in *Man and Society*, edited by Emerson P. Schmidt. New York: Prentice-Hall.

———. 1969. *Symbolic Interactionism*. Englewood Cliffs, NJ: Prentice-Hall.

Bottomore, Tom. 1984. *The Frankfurt School*. London: Tavistock.

Brown, Stephanie. 1985. *Treating the Alcoholic: A Developmental Model of Recovery*. New York: John Wiley.

Bruner, Edward M. 1986. "Experience and Its Expressions." Pp. 3-30 in *The Anthropology of Experience*, edited by Victor W. Turner and Edward M. Bruner. Urbana: University of Illinois Press.

Caddy, G. R., H. J. Addington, and D. Perkins. 1978. "Individualized Behavior Therapy for Alcoholics: A Third Year Independent Double-Bind Follow-Up." *Behavior Research and Therapy* 16:345-62.

Cavan, Sheri. 1974. "Seeing Social Structure in a Rural Setting." *Urban Life and Culture* 3:329-46.

Cho, Joo, Hyun. 1987. "A Social Phenomenological Understanding of Family Violence: The Case of Korea." Ph.D. dissertation, University of Illinois, Urbana, Department of Sociology.

———. 1988. *Battered Wives: Violence and Ressentiment in the Korean Family*. New York: Aldine de Gruyter.

Clifford, James. 1986. "Introduction: Partial Truths." Pp. 1-26 in *Writing Culture: The Poetics and Politics of Ethnography*, edited by James Clifford and George E. Marcus. Berkeley: University of California Press.

Clifford, James and George E. Marcus, eds. 1986. *Writing Culture: The Poetics and Politics of Ethnography*. Berkeley: University of California Press.

Coleridge, S. T. 1973. "Biographia Literaria." In *Major British Poets of the Romantic Period*, edited by W. Heath. New York: Macmillan. [Originally published 1817]

Collins, Randall. 1975. *Conflict Sociology: Toward an Explanatory Science*. New York: Academic Press.

Cook, Judith A. and Mary Margaret Fonow. 1986. "Knowledge and Women's Interests: Issues of Epistemology and Methodology in Feminist Sociological Research." *Sociological Inquiry* 56(Winter):2-29.

Couch, Carl J. 1984. *Constructing Civilizations.* Greenwich, CT: JAI Press.

———. Forthcoming. "Towards the Isolation of Elements of Social Structures." In *Studies in Symbolic Interaction*, Vol. 10. Greenwich, CT: JAI Press.

———, Stanley L. Saxton, and Michael A. Katovich, eds. 1986a. *Studies in Symbolic Interaction.* Supplement 2: *The Iowa School, Part A.* Greenwich, CT: JAI Press.

———. 1986b. *Studies in Symbolic Interaction.* Supplement 2: *The Iowa School, Part B.* Greenwich, CT: JAI Press.

Cowley, Malcolm, ed. 1967. "Introduction." In *The Portable Faulkner Reader*, revised and expanded edition. New York: Viking. [Originally published 1945]

Crapanzano, Vincent. 1980. *Tuhami: Portrait of a Moroccan.* Chicago: University of Chicago Press.

———. 1986. "Heremes' Dilemma: The Masking of Subversion in Ethnographic Description." Pp. 51-76 in *Writing Culture: The Poetics and Politics of Ethnography*, edited by James Clifford and George E. Marcus. Berkeley: University of California Press.

Culler, Jonathan. 1981. *The Pursuit of Signs: Semiotics, Literature, Deconstruction.* Ithaca, NY: Cornell University Press.

Davies, D. L. 1962. "Normal Drinking in Recovered Alcoholics." *Quarterly Journal of Studies on Alcohol* 23:94-104.

Denzin, Norman K. 1977. "Notes on the Criminogenic Hypothesis: A Case Study of the American Liquor Industry." *American Sociological Review* 42:905-20.

———. 1978. *The Research Act: A Theoretical Introduction to Sociological Methods.* 2nd edition. New York: McGraw-Hill. [Originally published 1970]

———. 1982a. "Contributions of Anthropology and Sociology to Qualitative Research Methods." Pp. 17-26 in *New Directions for Institutional Research: Qualitative Methods for Institutional Research*, edited by E. Kuhns and S. V. Martona. San Francisco: Jossey-Bass.

———. 1982b. "Notes on Criminology and Criminality." Pp. 115-30 in *Rethinking Criminology*, edited by H. E. Pepinsky. Beverly Hills, CA: Sage.

———. 1983. "Interpretive Interactionism." Pp. 129-46 in *Beyond Method: Strategies for Social Research*, edited by Gareth Morgan. Beverly Hills, CA: Sage.

———. 1984a. *On Understanding Emotion.* San Francisco: Jossey-Bass.

———. 1984b. "Toward a Phenomenology of Domestic, Family Violence." *American Journal of Sociology* 90(November):483-513.

———. 1986a. "Interpreting the Lives of Ordinary People: Sartre, Heidegger, Faulkner." *Life Stories/Recits de vie* 2:6-20.

———. 1986b. "Interpretive Interactionism and the Use of Life Histories." *Revista Internacional de Sociologia* 44:321-37.

———. 1987a. *The Alcoholic Self.* Beverly Hills, CA: Sage.

———. 1987b. *The Recovering Alcoholic.* Beverly Hills, CA: Sage.

———. 1987c. "On Semiotics and Symbolic Interaction." *Symbolic Interaction* 10(Spring):1-20.

———. 1987d. *Treating Alcoholism.* Beverly Hills, CA: Sage.

———. 1988. "Blue Velvet: Postmodern Contradictions." *Theory, Culture and Society* 5:461-73.

————. Forthcoming-a. *The Research Act*. Englewood Cliffs, NJ: Prentice-Hall.

————. Forthcoming-b. *Film and the American Alcoholic*. New York: Aldine de Gruyter.

————. Forthcoming-c. "Tender Mercies: Two Interpretations." *Sociological Quarterly* 30.

Derrida, Jacques. 1981. *Positions*. Chicago: University of Chicago Press.

Dilthey, W. L. 1976. *Selected Writings*. Cambridge: Cambridge University Press. [Originally published 1900]

Dolby-Stahl, Sandra K. 1985. "A Literary Folkloristic Methodology for the Study of Meaning in Personal Narrative." *Journal of Folklore Research* 22(January-April):45-70.

Dostoyevsky, Fyodor. 1950. *Crime and Punishment*. New York: Vintage. [Originally published 1864]

Dougherty, Janet W. D. 1985. "Introduction." Pp. 3-14 in *Directions in Cognitive Anthropology*, edited by J.W.D. Dougherty. Urbana: University of Illinois Press.

Douglas, Jack D. 1976. *Investigative Social Research: Individual and Team Field Research*. Beverly Hills, CA: Sage.

————. 1985. *Creative Interviewing*. Beverly Hills, CA: Sage.

———— and John M. Johnson, eds. 1977. *Existential Sociology*. New York: Cambridge University Press.

Farberman, Harvey A. 1975. "A Criminogenic Market Structure: The Automobile Industry." *Sociological Quarterly* 6:438-57.

———— and R. S. Perinbanayagam, eds. 1985. *Studies in Symbolic Interaction*. Supplement 1: *1985 Foundations of Interpretive Sociology; Original Essays in Symbolic Interaction*. Greenwich, CT: JAI Press.

Farganis, Sondra. 1986. "Social Theory and Feminist Theory: The Need for Dialogue." *Sociological Inquiry* 56(Winter):50-68.

Faris, Robert E.L. 1967. *Chicago Sociology: 1920-1932*. San Francisco: Chandler.

Faulkner, William. 1940. *The Hamlet*. New York: Vintage.

————. 1957. *The Town*. New York: Vintage.

————. 1959. *The Mansion*. New York: Vintage.

————. 1967. "Address Upon Receiving the Nobel Prize for Literature." Pp. 723-24 in *The Portable Faulkner*, revised and expanded edition, edited by M. Cowley. New York: Viking.

Fielding, Nigel G. and Jane L. Fielding. 1986. *Linking Data*. Beverly Hills, CA: Sage.

Fish, Stanley. 1980. *Is There a Text in This Class?* Cambridge, MA: Harvard University Press.

Foucault, Michel. 1979. *Discipline and Punish: The Birth of the Prison*. New York: Vintage.

————. 1980. *Power/Knowledge: Selected Interviews and Other Writings: 1972-1977*. New York: Pantheon.

————. 1982. "Afterword: The Subject and Power." Pp. 222-36 in *Michel Foucault: Beyond Structuralism and Hermeneutics*, edited by H. Dreyfus and P. Rabinow. Chicago: University of Chicago Press.

Freud, Sigmund. 1965. *The Interpretation of Dreams*. New York: Avon. [Originally published 1900]

Gadamer, H. G. 1975. *Truth and Method*. London: Sheed and Ward.

————. 1976. *Philosophical Hermeneutics*. Berkeley: University of California Press.

Garfinkel, Harold. 1967. *Studies in Ethnomethodology*. Englewood Cliffs, NJ: Prentice-Hall.

————, M. Lynch, and E. Livingston. 1981. "The Work of a Discovering Science Constructed with Material from the Optically Discovered Pulsar." *Philosophy of the Social Sciences* 11:131-58.

Garrow, David J. 1986. *Bearing the Cross: Martin Luther King, Jr., and the Southern Christian Leadership Conference*. New York: William Morrow.

Geertz, Clifford. 1973. "Deep Play: Notes on the Balinese Cockfight." Pp. 412-53 in *The Interpretation of Cultures*. New York: Basic Books. [Originally published in *Daedalus* 101:1-37]

————. 1983. *Local Knowledge: Further Essays in Interpretive Anthropology*. New York: Basic Books.

————. 1988. *Works and Lives: The Anthropologist as Author*. Stanford, CA: Stanford University Press.

Giddens, Anthony. 1985. *The Constitution of Society*. Berkeley: University of California Press.

Goffman, Erving. 1959. *The Presentation of Self in Everyday Life*. New York: Doubleday.

————. 1961a. *Asylums*. New York: Doubleday.

————. 1961b. *Encounters*. Indianapolis: Bobbs-Merrill.

————. 1967. *Interaction Ritual*. New York: Doubleday.

————. 1971. *Relations in Public*. New York: Basic Books.

————. 1974. *Frame Analysis*. New York: Harper.

————. 1981. *Forms of Talk*. Philadelphia: University of Pennsylvania Press.

————. 1983. "The Interaction Order." *American Sociological Review* 48:1-17.

Gold, Raymond. 1958. "Roles in Sociological Field Observations." *Social Forces* 36:217-23.

Gordon, Gerald and Edward V. Morse. 1975. "Evaluation Research." *Annual Review of Sociology* 1:339-61.

Habermas, Jürgen. 1984. *The Theory of Communicative Action*. Vol. 1, *Reason and the Rationalization of Society*. Boston: Beacon. [Originally published 1981]

Hall, Peter M. 1985. "Asymmetric Relationships and the Process of Power." Pp. 307-44 in *Foundations of Interpretive Sociology: Original Essays in Symbolic Interaction*, edited by H. Farberman and R. S. Perinbanayagam. Greenwich, CT: JAI Press.

Hall, Stuart. 1980. "Cultural Studies and the Centre: Some Problematics and Problems." Pp. 1-49 in *Culture, Media and Language: Working Papers in Cultural Studies, 1972-1979*, edited by S. Hall et al. London: Hutchinson.

Heidegger, Martin. 1962. *Being and Time*. New York: Harper & Row. [Originally published 1927]

————. 1982. *The Basic Problems of Phenomenology*. Bloomington: Indiana University Press.

Henry, Jules. 1965. *Culture Against Man*. New York: Vintage.

Heyl, Barbara Sherman. 1979. *The Madam as Entrepreneur: Career Management in House Prostitution*. New Brunswick, NJ: Transaction.

House, Ernest W. 1980. *Evaluating With Validity*. Beverly Hills, CA: Sage.

Howe, Richard Herbert. 1984. "Early Office Proletariat? A Reconstruction of Sears' Order Processing—1910." Pp. 155-70 in *Studies in Symbolic Interaction: A Research Annual*. Vol. 5, edited by N. K. Denzin. Greenwich, CT: JAI Press.

Husserl, E. 1962. *Ideas: General Introduction to Pure Phenomenology*. New York: Collier. [Originally published 1913]

James, William. 1950. *The Principles of Psychology*. New York: Dover. [Originally published 1890]

———. 1955. *Pragmatism and Four Essays from the Meaning of Truth*. New York: Humanities Press.

Jansen, Golieda G. 1988. "I Learned It from Real Life: Perspectives on Work and Self of Female Southeast Asian Paraprofessional Adjustment Workers." Ph.D. dissertation, University of Illinois, Urbana-Champaign, School of Social Work.

Jellinek, E. M. 1962. "Phases of Alcohol Addiction." Pp. 356-68 in *Society, Culture and Drinking Patterns*, edited by D. J. Pittman and C. R. Snyder. New York: John Wiley.

Johnson, John M. 1975. *Doing Field Research*. New York: Free Press.

———. 1977. "Ethnomethodology and Existential Sociology." Pp. 153-73 in *Existential Sociology*, edited by Jack D. Douglas and John M. Johnson. New York: Cambridge University Press.

——— and Kathleen J. Ferraro. 1984. "The Victimized Self: The Case of Battered Women." Pp. 119-30 in *The Existential Self in Society*, edited by Joseph A. Kotarba and Andrea Fontana. Chicago: University of Chicago Press.

Jordan, Glenn H. 1987. "On Subjects and Objects and Intertextuality: A Dialogue with Howard Spring and 'the New Cultural Anthropology.'" Presented to the 86th Annual Meeting of the American Anthropological Association, Chicago, November 25.

Joyce, James. 1976. "Dubliners." In *The Portable James Joyce*, edited by Harry Levin. New York: Penguin.

Kafka, Franz. 1952. *Selected Short Stories of Franz Kafka*. New York: Random House.

Kakutani, Michiko. 1987. "John Huston's Last Legacy." *New York Times* (Sunday, December 13): 1, 50.

Katovich, Michael A., Stanley L. Saxton, and Joel O. Powell. 1986. "Naturalism in the Laboratory." Pp. 79-88 in *Studies in Symbolic Interaction*. Supplement 2: *The Iowa School, Part A*. Greenwich, CT: JAI Press.

Klapp, Orrin E. 1964. *Symbolic Leaders: Public Dramas and Public Men*. Chicago: Aldine.

Kotarba, Joseph A. and Andrea Fontana, eds. 1984. *The Existential Self in Society*. Chicago: University of Chicago Press.

Kurtz, Ernest. 1979. *Not-God: A History of Alcoholics Anonymous*. Center City, MN: Hazelden Educational Materials.

Laing, R. D. 1965. *The Divided Self: An Existential Study in Sanity and Madness*. Harmondsworth, England: Penguin.

Leach, Barry and John L. Norris. 1977. "Factors in the Development of Alcoholics Anonymous (A.A.)." Pp. 441-519 in *The Biology of Alcoholism*. Vol. 5, *Treatment and Rehabilitation of the Chronic Alcoholic*, edited by Benjamin Kissin and Henri Beglieter. New York: Plenum.

Levin, Harry, ed. 1976. "Editor's Preface." Pp. 1-18 in *The Portable James Joyce*. New York: Penguin.

Lieberson, Stanley. 1985. *Making It Count: The Improvement of Social Theory and Research*. Berkeley: University of California Press.

Lincoln, Yvonne A. and Egon G. Guba. 1985. *Naturalistic Inquiry*. Beverly Hills, CA: Sage.

Lindesmith, Alfred R. 1947. *Opiate Addiction*. Bloomington, IN: Principia Press.

———. 1952. "Comment on W. S. Robinson's 'The Logical Structure of Analytic Induction.'" *American Sociological Review* 17:492-93.

———, Anselm L. Strauss, and Norman K. Denzin. 1988. *Social Psychology*. Englewood Cliffs, NJ: Prentice-Hall.

Lofland, John. 1971. *Analyzing Social Settings*. Belmont, CA: Wadsworth.

——— and Lyn H. Lofland. 1984. *Analyzing Social Settings*. Belmont, CA: Wadsworth.

Lyotard, Jean-Francois. 1984. *The Postmodern Condition: A Report on Knowledge*. Minneapolis: University of Minnesota Press.

Madsen, William. 1974. *The American Alcoholic*. Springfield, IL: Charles C Thomas.

Majchrzak, Ann. 1984. *Methods for Policy Research*. Beverly Hills, CA: Sage.

Manning, Peter K. 1987. *Semiotics and Fieldwork*. Newbury Park, CA: Sage.

———. 1988. "Semiotics and Social Psychology." *Studies in Symbolic Interaction* 9(Part A):153-80.

Marcus, George E. and Michael M.J. Fischer. 1986. *Anthropology as Cultural Critique: An Experimental Moment in the Human Sciences*. Chicago: University of Chicago Press.

Marx, Karl. 1983. "From the Eighteenth Brumaire of Louis Bonaparte." Pp. 287-323 in *The Portable Karl Marx*, edited by E. Kamenka. New York: Penguin. [Originally published 1852]

Maxwell, Milton A. 1984. *The Alcoholics Anonymous Experience: A Close-Up View for Professionals*. New York: McGraw-Hill.

Mead, George Herbert. 1934. *Mind, Self and Society*. Chicago: University of Chicago Press.

Mellow, Nancy K. 1972. "Behavioral Studies of Alcoholism." Pp. 219-92 in *The Biology of Alcoholism*. Vol. 2, *Physiology and Behavior*, edited by Benjamin Kissin and Henri Beglieter. New York: Plenum.

Merleau-Ponty, Maurice. 1962. *The Phenomenology of Perception*. Atlantic Highlands, NJ: Humanities Press.

———. 1964. *The Primacy of Perception*. Evanston, IL: Northwestern University Press.

———. 1968. *The Visible and the Invisible*. Evanston, IL: Northwestern University Press.

———. 1973a. *The Prose of the World*. Evanston, IL: Northwestern University Press.

———. 1973b. *Adventures of the Dialectic*. Evanston, IL: Northwestern University Press.

Merton Robert K. and Patricia Kendall. 1946. "The Focused Interview." *American Journal of Sociology* 51:541-57.

Mills, C. Wright. 1959. *The Sociological Imagination*. New York: Oxford University Press.

Mulford, Harold. 1986. "The Alcohol Problem: The Doctor Has Arrived, Now What?" Presented to the 1986 Annual Meetings of the Midwest Sociological Association, Des Moines, Iowa, March 29.

Nelson, Cary, ed. 1986. *Theory in the Classroom*. Urbana: University of Illinois Press.

Pattison, E. Mansell. 1966. "A Critique of Alcoholism Treatment Concepts." *Quarterly Journal of Studies on Alcohol* 27:49-71.

———, E. B. Headley, G. C. Gleser, and L. A. Gottschalk. 1968. "Abstinence and Normal Drinking: An Assessment of Changes in Drinking Patterns in Alcoholics After Treatment." *Quarterly Journal of Studies on Alcohol* 29:610-33.

Patton, Michael Quinn. 1980. *Qualitative Evaluation Methods*. Beverly Hills, CA: Sage.

———. 1981. *Creative Evaluation*. Beverly Hills, CA: Sage.

———. 1982. *Practical Evaluation*. Beverly Hills, CA: Sage.

Peirce, Charles Sanders. 1934. *Collected Papers of Charles Sanders Peirce*, Vols. 5 and 6. Cambridge, MA: Harvard University Press.

————. 1963. *Collected Papers of Charles Sanders Peirce*. Vols. 7 and 8. Cambridge, MA: Harvard University Press.

Pendery, Mary L., Irving M. Maltzman, and L. Jolyn West. 1982. "Controlled Drinking by Alcoholics: New Findings and a Reevaluation of a Major Affirmative Study." *Science* 217:169-75.

Perinbanayagam, R. S. 1985. *Signifying Acts*. Carbondale: Southern Illinois University Press.

Pike, Kenneth. 1954. *Language in Relation to an Unified Theory of the Structure of Human Behavior*. Vol. 1. Glendale, CA: Summer Institute of Linguistics.

Plummer, Ken. 1983. *Life Documents*. London: Unwin.

Rabinow, Paul. 1986. "Representations Are Social Facts: Modernity and Post-Modernity in Anthropology." Pp. 234-61 in *Writing Culture: The Poetics and Politics of Ethnography*, edited by James Clifford and George E. Marcus. Berkeley: University of California Press.

Rail, Genevieve. Forthcoming. "A Phenomenological Study of Physical Contact in Women's Varsity Basketball." Ph.D. dissertation, University of Illinois, Urbana-Champaign, Department of Kinesiology.

Raines, Howell. 1986. "Review of *Bearing the Cross: Martin Luther King Jr. and the Southern Christian Leadership Conference* [by David J. Garrow]." *New York Review of Books* (November 30): 133-34.

Ricoeur, Paul. 1979. "The Model of the Text: Meaningful Action Considered as a Text." Pp. 73-101 in *Interpretive Social Science: A Reader*, edited by Paul Rabinow and William M. Sullivan. Berkeley: University of California Press.

————. 1985. *Time and Narrative*. Vol. 2. Chicago: University of Chicago Press.

Rosaldo, Renato. 1984. "Grief and a Headhunter's Rage: On the Cultural Force of Emotions." Pp. 178-98 in *Text, Play, and Story: The Construction and Reconstruction of Self and Society*, edited by Edward M. Bruner. Washington, DC: American Ethnological Society.

————. 1986. "Ilongot Hunting as Story and Experience." Pp. 97-138 in *The Anthropology of Experience*, edited by Victor W. Turner and Edward M. Bruner. Urbana: University of Illinois Press.

Rose, Edward. 1988. "The Gloss: An Elementary Form of Social Life." Presented to the 1988 Annual Meetings of the Midwest Sociological Society, Minneapolis, Minnesota, March 25.

Rubington, Earl. 1973. *Alcohol Problems and Social Control*. Columbus, OH: Charles E. Merrill.

Rudy, David. 1986. *Becoming an Alcoholic*. Carbondale: Southern Illinois University Press.

Ryle, Gilbert. 1968. *The Thinking of Thoughts*. University Lectures, no. 18. Saskatoon: University of Saskatchewan.

Sartre, Jean-Paul. 1948. *The Psychology of Imagination*. New York: Philosophical Library.

————. 1956. *Being and Nothingness*. New York: Philosophical Library. [Originally published 1943]

————. 1963. *Search for a Method*. New York: Knopf.

————. 1972. *Imagination: A Psychological Critique*. Ann Arbor: University of Michigan Press. [Originally published 1940]

————. 1976. *Critique of Dialectical Reason*. London: NLP.

———. 1981. *The Family Idiot: Gustave Flaubert, 1821-1857*. Vol. 1. Chicago: University of Chicago Press.

Saussure, F. de. 1959. *The Course in General Linguistics*. New York: McGraw-Hill.

Schatzman, Leonard and Anselm L. Strauss. 1973. *Field Research: Strategies for a Natural Sociology*. Englewood Cliffs, NJ: Prentice-Hall.

Scheler, Max. 1961. *Ressentiment*, edited by L. Coser, translated by W. H. Holdeim. New York: Free Press. [Originally published 1912]

Schuckit, Marc and Jane Duby. 1983. "Alcoholism in Women." Pp. 215-42 in *The Biology of Alcoholism*. Vol. 6, *Psychological Factors*, edited by Benjamin Kissin and Henri Begleiter. New York: Plenum.

Schutz, Alfred. 1962. *Collected Papers*. Vol. 1, *The Problem of Social Reality*. The Hague, the Netherlands: Martinus Nijhoff.

———. 1964. *Collected papers*. Vol. 2, *Studies in Social Theory*. The Hague, the Netherlands: Martinus Nijhoff.

Shaw, Clifford. 1966. *The Jack-Roller*. Chicago: University of Chicago Press.

Silverman, David. 1985. *Qualitative Methodology & Sociology: Describing the Social World*. Hants, England, and Brookfield, VT: Gower.

Sobell, Linda, Mark B. Sobell, and Elliot Ward. 1980. *Evaluating Alcohol and Drug Abuse Treatment Effectiveness: Recent Advances*. New York: Pergamon.

Sobell, Mark B. and Linda C. Sobell. 1978. *Behavioral Treatment of Alcohol Problems: Individualized Therapy and Controlled Drinking*. New York: Plenum.

Stake, Robert E. 1978. "The Case-Study Method of Social Inquiry." *Educational Researcher* 7:5-8.

———. 1986. *Quieting Reform: Social Science and Social Action in an Urban Youth Program*. Urbana: University of Illinois Press.

Stone, Brad L. 1985. "Interpretive Sociology and the New Hermeneutics." Pp. 3-29 in *Studies in Symbolic Interaction: A Research Annual*. Vol. 6, edited by N. K. Denzin. Greenwich, CT: JAI Press.

Stone, Gregory P. 1981. "Appearance and the Self: A Slightly Revised Version." Pp. 187-202 in *Social Psychology Through Symbolic Interaction*, edited by G. P. Stone and H. A. Farberman. New York: John Wiley.

Strauss, Anselm L. 1959. *Mirrors and Masks: The Search for Identity*. Glencoe, IL: Free Press.

———. 1987. *Qualitative Analysis for Social Scientists*. New York: Cambridge University Press.

——— and Barney G. Glaser. 1970. *Anguish: A Case History of a Dying Trajectory*. Mill Valley, CA: Sociology Press.

Sudnow, David. 1978. *Ways of the Hand*. New York: Knopf.

———. 1979. *Talk's Body*. New York: Knopf.

Thomas, Dylan. 1964. *Adventures in the Skin Trade and Other Stories*. New York: New Directions. [Originally published 1938]

Thomas, W. I. and Florian Znaniecki. 1918-20. *The Polish Peasant in Europe and America*. 5 Vols. Boston: Richard G. Badger. [Vols. 1 and 2 originally published by the University of Chicago Press, 1918]

Thompson, Paul. 1978. *Voices of the Past: Oral History*. Oxford: Oxford University Press.

Tiebout, Harry M. 1944. "Therapeutic Mechanisms in Alcoholics Anonymous." *American Journal of Psychiatry* 100:468-73.

————. 1954. "The Ego Factor in Surrender to Alcoholism." *Quarterly Journal of Studies on Alcohol* 15:610-21.

Titon, Jeff Todd. 1980. "The Life Story." *Journal of American Folklore* 93(July-September):276-92.

Tompkins, Jane P., ed. 1980. *Reader-Response Criticism*. Baltimore: Johns Hopkins University Press.

Travisano, Richard. 1985. "Alternation and Conversion as Qualitatively Different Transformation." Pp. 237-48 in *Social Psychology Through Symbolic Interaction*, edited by G. P. Stone and H. A. Farberman. New York: John Wiley.

Treichler, Paula, ed. 1985. *For Alma Mater: Theory and Practice in Feminist Scholarship*. Urbana: University of Illinois Press.

Turner, Victor W. 1986. "Dewey, Dilthey, and Drama: An Essay in the Anthropology of Experience." Pp. 33-44 in *The Anthropology of Experience*, edited by Victor W. Turner and Edward M. Bruner. Urbana: University of Illinois Press.

———— and Edward M. Bruner, eds. 1986. *The Anthropology of Experience*. Urbana: University of Illinois Press.

Vaughan, Diane. 1986. *Uncoupling: Turning Points in Intimate Relationships*. New York: Oxford University Press.

Weber, Max. 1977. *Critique of Stammler*. New York: Free Press.

Wiley, Norbert. 1986. "Early American Sociology and The Polish Peasant." *Sociological Theory* 4:20-39.

Wittgenstein, Ludwig. 1922. *Tractacus Logico-Philosophicus*. London: Routledge & Kegan Paul.

Yin, Robert K. 1985. *Case Study Research*. Beverly Hills, CA: Sage.

NAME INDEX

SUBJECT INDEX

ABOUT THE AUTHOR

Norman K. Denzin is Professor of Sociology and Humanities at the University of Illinois at Urbana-Champaign. He received a B.A. degree (1963) and a Ph.D. degree (1966) in sociology from the University of Iowa. Denzin's main research activities and interests have been in childhood socialization, the study of language, the self, interaction, interpretive theory, and phenomenology. He has been Vice-President of the Society for the Study of Symbolic Interaction (1976-1977), Secretary of the Social Psychology Section of the American Sociological Association (1978-1980), and in 1987, was elected President of the Midwest Sociological Society. He is the author and editor of several books, including *Social Psychology* (1988, with A. Lindesmith and S. Strauss, 6th edition), *Sociological Methods* (1978), *The Research Act* (1989, 3rd edition), *Childhood Socialization* (1977), *Children and Their Caretakers* (1973), *The Values of Social Science* (1973), *The Mental Patient* (1968, with S. P. Spitzer), *On Understanding Emotion* (1984), *The Recovering Alcoholic* (1987), *The Alcoholic Self* (1987), and *Interpretive Interactionism* (1989). His book, *The Alcoholic Self*, won the Charles Horton Cooley award in 1988 by the Society for the Study of Symbolic Interaction. He is the editor of *Studies in Symbolic Interaction: A Research Annual* and the author of over fifty articles, which have appeared in such journals as *American Journal of Sociology, American Sociological Review, British Journal of Sociology, Semiotica, Social Forces, Social Problems, and Sociological Quarterly*.